# THE
# LITTLE
# BOOK
## OF
# SHROPSHIRE

### JOHN SHIPLEY

First published 2015
Reprinted 2016

The History Press
The Mill, Brimscombe Port
Stroud, Gloucestershire, GL5 2QG
www.thehistorypress.co.uk

British Library Cataloguing in Publication Data.
A catalogue record for this book is available from the British Library.

ISBN 978 0 7509 6064 9

Typesetting and origination by The History Press
Printed in Turkey by Imak.

# CONTENTS

# INTRODUCTION

Many counties may lay claim to the title of the prettiest in England, but despite their many and undoubted charms, few can aspire to the unique diversity to be found in the county of Shropshire.

Take an extended walk through what has been called 'The Secret County' and along the way you will discover timeless villages with ancient churches, historic abbeys and castles, a Roman city, breath-taking views, colourful market towns, teashops and numerous country inns. The county is home to not one but two UNESCO World Heritage Sites: the Ironbridge Gorge, and the Pontcysyllte Aqueduct and Canal.

This *Little Book of Shropshire* is a vibrant, fast-paced, fact-packed compendium of compelling information filled with the frivolous and fantastic, unbelievable and downright strange details about the county of Shropshire. It includes a plethora of eccentric individuals who have inhabited Shropshire, its famous sons and daughters, heroes and villains, royal connections and a pile of facts about Shropshire's history, its beautiful landscape, towns and villages, plus a collection of bizarre historical trivia. All this comes together in an easy-to-carry pocket-sized book that is essential reading for visitors and locals alike.

The ceremonial border county of Shropshire, estimated population in 2011 of 473,900, separates much of central England from Mid-Wales, an area that in older, more violent times was policed by a group of noblemen known as 'The Marcher Lords'.

In England, the county shares borders with Cheshire, Staffordshire, Worcestershire and Herefordshire, and in Wales with Powys and Wrexham, covering an area of 1,346 square miles (3,487 sq km).

The snaking River Severn, Britain's longest river, divides the county and, together with the western hills and the mysterious and evocative

BUTCHER  ROW
SHREWSBURY

Offa's Dyke, has for centuries provided a natural barrier to racial conflict. The other major river in the county is the Teme.

Within the timeless Shropshire landscapes there are charming market towns, each with its own distinctive character, such as: Ellesmere, Market Drayton, Oswestry, Bishops Castle, Ludlow, Much Wenlock and Bridgnorth. Among enticing streets and alleyways you will find antique and craft shops, inns and teashops rubbing shoulders with traditional grocers, butchers and bakers.

In the very heart of Shropshire lies the historic county town of Shrewsbury, one of the finest Tudor towns in England, and to the east – in the UNESCO World Heritage Site of Ironbridge – the ten museums of the Ironbridge Gorge celebrate the birthplace of the Industrial Revolution.

So whether you're seeking horticultural sanctuary or historical stimulation, amusement or distraction, Shropshire has something for everyone: award-winning museums, renowned gardens, distinctive National Trust and English Heritage properties, fascinating farm attractions, abbeys and churches, street markets, speciality shops and craft centres, and unspoilt countryside to explore.

My wife and I have lived in Bridgnorth since 1968 – having emigrated from Wednesbury in the Black Country – raised a family and now call the place home. Bridgnorth was one of the riverside places that Black Country people came to for their holidays. My family did. I first fell in love with my adopted county on these annual holidays, but never dreamt I would have the chance to live here.

Collecting information and assembling this book has given me much pleasure. I hope that reading it will give you even more enjoyment.

*John Shipley, 2015*

# ACKNOWLEDGEMENTS

I would like to take this opportunity to publicly thank and acknowledge all the people, individuals and organisations who have helped with the compilation of material for this book and without whom the project could not have been completed: international ice hockey legend and percussionist supreme Chuck Taylor; television's Gary Newbon; Adrian Pearce of the Shropshire History website (www.shropshirehistory.com); Sarah Davis, Archivist at Shropshire Archives; Martin Davis and David Gittins at Shrewsbury Railway Heritage Trust; Elizabeth Bailey, Secretary of the Dawley History Group; the Shropshire Library Service; the staff at Bridgnorth Public Library; Martin Wood, author and Shrewsbury Town Crier; the Ironbridge Gorge Museum Trust; the Broseley History Society; BBC Shropshire; and Anne Williams at the Bog Visitor Centre.

My son, Peter Shipley, for his immense contribution – rewrites, additional facts and proof checking. Plus, of course, my long-suffering, proofreading wife, Kate, and friends Eric Smith and Mike Thomas for their input.

And to Matilda Richards and Naomi Reynolds at The History Press.

The material for this book has been compiled and assembled from personal research, archive material, various websites and printed matter, and, of course, word of mouth, all of which has been used in good faith. The majority of illustrations are by the author; all others are The History Press's collection.

Whilst every effort has been made to check and recheck the facts and items in this book, the publisher and author bear no responsibility for the content. Where possible, permission has been sought.

And lastly, please forgive me if I have not included any of your particular favourite Shropshire facts.

# 1

# HOW IT
# ALL STARTED

Evidence from radiometric dating indicates that our Earth, formed by accretion from the solar nebula, is around 4,540 million (4.54 billion) years old, a lifespan that is divided into thirteen separate geological periods, eleven of which are represented in the modern-day county of Shropshire by different rocks and scenery. Just as a snapshot for comparison, Snowdonia has only three of these different periods.

The Precambrian period, covering all of Earth's history up to around 570 million years ago, is when Shropshire's oldest rocks were formed: volcanic ash and lava formed the hills known as the Wrekin and the Lawley, and Caer Caradoc, plus many others on the eastern side of the Church Stretton Valley, and Earl's Hill, near Pontesbury. Contrary to local popular belief, the Wrekin is not an extinct volcano, though it is made up of volcanic rock. Later in the Precambrian period, Shropshire was covered by a shallow sea, during which time the county's extensive sandstone beds, such as the Long Mynd plateau, were laid down.

Also during this period, a major break, or fault, appeared in the Earth's crust, known as the Church Stretton Fault – a line along which violent earthquakes occurred for many millions of years, but which has lain dormant for around 200 million years. Following this, during the Cambrian, Ordovician and Silurian periods, between c. 570 and c. 400 million years ago, the county lay almost continuously under the sea: shallow in the east, deeper in the west. Only the tops of the Long Mynd and Stiperstones would have been visible, standing out above the level of the water like islands.

One of the first inhabitants of the area was the lizard-like Rynchosaur, a diapsid reptile that grew up to 2m in length. This herbivore existed in the Triassic period around 240 million years ago. Fossils and footprints of this creature have been found in the county, the latter in a quarry at Grinshill.

Prior to the last Ice Age, what is now the River Severn flowed in the opposite direction, flowing northwards to the River Dee estuary, but of course the arrival of the ice froze up the flow, then, when the ice retreated, the meltwater that was left behind became trapped, forming a series of large lakes, eventually merging to form Lake Lapworth in present-day Leicestershire. When this lake overflowed, the water carved out the Ironbridge Gorge, creating a natural passage for the present course of the Severn.

During the last Ice Age, Shropshire was covered by a dense sheet of ice up to 300m thick until around 20,000 years ago. At this time the only part of today's county above the level of the ice was the Stiperstones Ridge.

Amazingly, in those far-off days great mammoths roamed the county. And to prove it, remains of these giant creatures were found in 1986 in a quarry at Condover. The oldest was dated to around 12,700 years old.

Between 4,000 and 2,500 BC, Britain was inhabited by Neolithic (new Stone Age) tribes, and there is evidence of farming in Shropshire at this time.

The earliest known example of a Stone Age settlement in Shropshire is thought to be the Roveries hill fort in the south-west of the county. Excavations have suggested that the hill was inhabited some 2,000 years before the Iron Age hill fort was constructed, as fragments of pottery and a hearth dating back to the Neolithic period were found.

Evidence of the existence of Stone Age residents in Shropshire can be seen in the numerous tumuli (stone burial chambers), plus the many standing stones and stone circles that are dotted around the county.

In Neolithic times anyone wishing to travel far kept well clear of the densely forested valleys, preferring the safer and easier crests of hills known as ridgeways. A fine example of this is the Portway, a major ridgeway across the Long Mynd, used by Neolithic axe traders, and still recognised as the King's Highway up until the Middle Ages.

The Clun area has seen the discovery of a plethora of artefacts: over 1,000 flint tools and weapons. It seems that the area around Clun was as popular then as it is today.

The Neolithic peoples were followed by bronze-using Celts, dwelling in huts or on artificial mounds surrounded by lakes or pools, such as those found at Berth, near Baschurch. Bronze implements have been found at Bagley, near Hordley, and dugout canoes have been found at Crose Mere and Marton Pool, near Chirbury.

In 54 BC Julius Caesar came across from Gaul and gave the indigenous peoples of our island the name Britons, whose distinctive circular fortifications seem to crown almost every hill in Shropshire, and can be found at Gaer Ditches, Titterstone, Abdon Burf and Bury Ditches.

At the time of the Roman invasion, Shropshire was most likely sparsely inhabited by the Cornovii, whose lands straddled much of the county, and the Ordovices in the west, mostly in Wales. The lands of the Cornovii are believed to have stretched from Merseyside down to the West Midlands, plus parts of Herefordshire – their capital may have been the hill fort on the Wrekin. Other impressive examples of their hill forts are at Old Oswestry and Bury Ditches, but upon dusting off your Ordinance Survey maps you will notice that there are hill forts all over Shropshire, possibly fifty or more.

Roman history of the county only really starts a century after Julius Caesar's landing. The Roman general Ostorius established fortified camps along the Severn Valley, but in Shropshire the Romans met with fierce resistance, particularly from the Ordovices.

It is believed that the famous British chieftain Caratacus of the Belgic Catuvellauni tribe, who led the resistance to the Roman invasion of Britain, may have suffered his final defeat in Shropshire at the Battle of Caer Caradoc. This may well have been fought on the hill of this name near Church Stretton. Other places in Shropshire and elsewhere, such as Briedden just across the county's north-west border, have been suggested for the site of this battle, however my personal favourite is Caer Caradoc with its ancient hill fort and incredible views (more about Caratacus and this battle later).

The Romans under the general Julius Agricola finally defeated the Ordovices in AD 78. The county lands thus passified, the Romans quickly settled into what they did best – building. Shropshire has a handful of Roman towns, the principle one being Viroconium

Cornoviorum (Wroxeter, near Shrewsbury), which became the fourth largest town of Roman Britain with a population of around 6,000 at its peak in the second century. Other principle towns were Mediolanum (Whitchurch) and Vxacona (Redhill, Oakengates). It's also worth mentioning the town of Bravonium (Leintwardine, Herefordshire), which is only a Roman mile or two from the Shropshire border.

There are many Roman roads in Shropshire, the most notable being Watling Street, which was originally an ancient British pathway route developed and paved over by the 14th Legion.

Of Roman Villas, that iconic insight into Roman rural life, there are traces, but sadly fewer than in more southern and eastern counties of the UK. Examples include Acton Scott, Yarchester near Wenlock, Lea Cross near Pontesbury, Ashford Carbonell near Ludlow, Cruckton near Shrewsbury and Whitley Grange near Shrewsbury. Traces of other Roman buildings have been discovered at Oakengates (Vxacona), Bury Walls near Hawkstone, Old Oswestry, Linley, Stanton Lacy and Rushbury. Fortified posts probably of Roman date can be found at Norton Camp on Whettlebury Hill, Nordy Bank, Chesterton Walls, Llanymynech, Caynham, Edbury Camp near Haughmond and possibly Wall Camp near Kinnersley.

The Romans used slaves to mine lead on the Stiperstones, and copper and lead at Llanymynech.

Much of what we know today about Roman Britain comes from the writings of the celebrated Roman geographer and astrologer, Claudius Ptolemaeus, who lived

STANTON LACY

in the second century AD, during the reigns of Emperors Hadrian and Antonine. Ptolemaeus, more widely known as Ptolemy, was Greek by descent, but hailed from the Egyptian city of Alexandria. He published several books on astronomy, but his seven-volume work *Geographia*, became the standard textbook on all things geographical until the fifteenth century. The British Isles are mentioned early in volume two. In chapter two, entitled 'Albion island of Britannia', Ptolemy describes mainland Britain, listing major landmarks, the coastline, rivers and estuaries, the names of the British tribes and the names of their principal towns. He also tells us the names of the neighbouring tribes of the Cornovii: the Brigantes to the north-east, the Corianti to the east, the Dobunni to the south, the Demetae to the west and the Deceangi in the north-west. (The poor old Ordovices don't get a mention.)

He and other Roman writers have also given us the names of the larger rivers:

- *Seteia Aestuarium* (the Mersey), which formed the natural border between the lands of the Cornovii and the Brigantes.
- *Deva Fluvius* (the Dee), which, with the next two names, come directly from the Latin.
- *Trisantona Fluvius* (the Trent).
- *Sabrina Fluvius* (the Severn).

He also tells us that the principle tribal centre was at *Civitas Cornoviorum* (*Viroconium Cornoviorum*, or Wroxeter if you prefer).

After the Romans abandoned Britain around AD 410, Angle and Saxon invaders from Northern Germany and Denmark filled the power vacuum and began to settle in Britain. One of the invading tribes established the Kingdom of Mercia, which incorporated modern-day Shropshire, centred around Staffordshire, with its capital at Tamworth. Unfortunately, not much is known after this until AD 577, when Ceawlin, King of Wessex marched north up the Severn Valley. Then in AD 584, a force of West Saxons sacked and destroyed Viroconium, attacking again in AD 661 and defeating the Mercians in a great battle at Pontesbury.

The Saxons left their mark on the county in the form of place names:

- Tun (a settlement) such as at Culmington (the tun of Culming)
- Ley (a clearing) such as at Billingsley
- Hall (a house/dwelling) such as at Bonninghall
- Wardine (an estate) such as at Shrawardine (the estate of the sheriff)

During the period AD 500–850, often referred to as 'The Dark Ages', a number of Anglo-Saxon kingdoms were established. From AD 527–879 Shropshire was part of the Kingdom of Mercia, one of seven kingdoms known collectively as the Heptarchy (this term derived from the Greek has been in use since the sixteenth century). The other six were Northumbria, East Anglia, Essex, Kent, Sussex and Wessex.

From AD 879–918 Mercia was an independent kingdom, after that it became a client state of Wessex.

The two Mercian peoples were the Hecani in the west, later known as the Magonsaete (those that lived around Magana/Maud Bryan in Herefordshire) and the Wreocensaete (who lived around the Wrekin).

The new shire of Shropshire was created some time between AD 900 and 925 as part of the defence of English Mercia against the Danes, who had settled in eastern England.

Having looked at our ancient beginnings, let's turn our attention to how the county got its name ...

MERCIAN WAY MILE MARKER

## WHAT'S IN A NAME?

A lot of people I know – those who harbour the misguided idea that I might know a thing or two, and probably loads who think I don't – ask me how to pronounce the name of our beloved county town (which, incidentally, in my humble view, should be a city). Let me say right off that as a bloke born and bred in the Black Country, a place where we say most English words incorrectly, I am the wrong chap to ask.

The debate continues: does one pronounce it Shrewsbury (with the 'ew' as in 'sew', or as in 'shrew' – the small long-nosed rodent), or Shroesbury, Shrewsbry, Shewsbury, Shewsbry, Shoesbry or Shrowsbury (with the 'ow' as in show)? And so it goes on.

I have lived in Bridgnorth for almost fifty years, and in that time I have heard all of these pronunciations, and some of them have been used on maps in the past. So which pronunciation is correct? Probably all of them. I will have to leave it to the individual reader to decide; begging forgiveness if I missed out your favourite.

The name Shropshire is derived from the Old English word 'Shrobbesbyrigscir', which means Shrewsburyshire – in the *Anglo-Saxon Annals* it was 'Scrobbesbyrig-scyre' and 'Scrobb-scire'. Later writers called it 'Scrop-scire', and 'Salopschire' and subsequently 'Schropshire'.

The Old English name for Shrewsbury was 'Scrobbesburh' or 'Scrobbesbyrig', meaning 'fort in the scrub-land region'; or 'Scrobb's fort', meaning 'shrubstown' or 'the town of the bushes'. This name gradually evolved in three directions, into 'Sciropscire', which morphed into Shropshire; into 'Sloppesberie', which became Salop/Salopia (an alternative name for both town and county); and from 'Ciropsberie' into 'Schrosberie', which eventually became the town's name, Shrewsbury. The Normans called it 'Salopsberia' or 'Salopescira'. In 1888 the county council was known as Salop County Council, but in 1980 this was changed to Shropshire County Council. Salop is no longer used.

The Shropshire dialect is not heard so much these days, but not so long ago its distinctive vocabulary and accent was present throughout the county. Here are just a few Shropshire colloquialisms to provide a flavour of the dialect:

| | |
|---|---|
| Aunti-praunty | High spirited |
| Acker (ak'ur') | To tremble with passion |
| Badger (bajur) | A huckster or middleman |
| Barley child | A child born out of wedlock |
| Castrel (kastrel) | A worthless person |
| Chit-up | A forward girl |
| Dacky (daki) | A suckling pig |
| Daggly | Showery weather |
| Fumey | Passionate, hasty |
| Fussock | A big, dirty, greasy woman |

| | |
|---|---|
| Gammocks | Rough play |
| Gid | A dizziness that sheep are liable to |
| Gird | To pull violently |
| Noggling | Bungling, blundering |
| Onder | Afternoon |
| Onshooty | Uneven |
| Oontyump | A molehill |
| Poon | Hit |
| Potch | To poke, to thrust, to make a hole |
| Quank | Still, quiet |
| Quite | A woodpigeon |
| Sclemgut | To be greedy |

# 2

# PLACES

The ten largest towns in Shropshire by population are:

- Telford (incorporating the towns of Wellington, Oakengates, Madeley and Dawley), estimated at between 166,600 and 171,700
- Shrewsbury, 71,715
- Oswestry, 15,613
- Bridgnorth, 12,212
- Newport, 10,814
- Ludlow, 10,500
- Market Drayton, 10,407
- Whitchurch, 8,907
- Shifnal, 7,094
- Wem, 5,142

## SOME FACTS ABOUT SHROPSHIRE'S MAJOR TOWNS AND PLACES

(The names given in Domesday Book are in parentheses)

**Telford:** The largest town in the county, the 'new town' of Telford is really a collection of towns – Wellington, Madeley, Oakengates and Dawley – created in the 1960s and 1970s, with a combined estimated population in the borough of 170,300 in 2010, 155,000 in Telford itself. The town is of course named after the legendary civil engineer Thomas Telford, and includes the Ironbridge Gorge UNESCO World Heritage Site. Incidentally, the new town might never have been named Telford; other suggestions were

Dawelloak and Wrekin Forest City. In the early medieval period, coal and ironstone mining brought a higher level of development and prosperity to the area. Both Madeley (Madelie) and Dawley (Dalelie) are mentioned in Domesday Book.

**Shrewsbury (Ciroposberie):** Shropshire's county town lies in a great loop of the River Severn. The settlement was founded by the Saxons, but it wasn't until Tudor times that the town was extensively developed. Shrewsbury is a town of quaint winding alleyways and streets, framed by half-timbered medieval houses, many from the fifteenth and sixteenth centuries. The skyline of this beautiful and historic market town is crowned by a castle and a host of church spires, plus a former Benedictine monastery that is now an abbey. There are wonderful parks and open spaces to enjoy and the town boasts well over 600 historic listed buildings. The old red sandstone Norman castle was founded in 1074 by Roger de Montgomery, the first Earl of Shrewsbury. It is believed that Anglo-Saxon Shrewsbury was most probably a settlement fortified through the use of earthworks comprising a ditch and rampart, which were then shored up with a wooden stockade. The first written reference to Shrewsbury dates back to 901. It refers to 'Scrobbesbyrig', which indicates that it was then a fortified settlement: 'byrig', with 'Scrobbes', most likely referring to a scrub-covered hill.

The town hosts the annual Shrewsbury Flower Show, one of the oldest and largest horticultural events in the country, and is known for its floral displays, having won various awards since the turn of the twenty-first century, including Britain in Bloom in 2006.

**Oswestry (Luure):** Oswestry is one of the county's oldest border settlements. Named after Oswald, who was both a king and a saint, Oswestry is the largest market town and civil parish in the county. The town is built around Saint Oswald's church, and is situated only 5 miles from the border with Wales. Oswestry has always been a centre for trade and drew Welsh woollen merchants, resulting in a mixed English and Welsh heritage.

**Bridgnorth:** The town of Bridgnorth has many unique features. Split into two distinct communities on either bank of the River

Severn, High Town and Low Town are connected by a bridge designed and built by the great civil engineer Thomas Telford. Earlier names for the settlement include Brigge, Brug and Bruges. The earliest reference to a settlement dates to AD 895, when it is recorded that the Danes had set up a camp at Cwatbridge, now Quatford, a couple of miles downstream from Bridgnorth where there was a river crossing. The first mention of a bridge came fifteen years later, in AD 910, however the exact site is not known. Two years after this, King Alfred's daughter, Æthelfleda, the lady of Mercia, built a castle, most probably a fortified mound, at a place called Bridge on the west bank of the River Severn. The Norman Conquest in 1066 saw Bridgnorth grow in importance when the manor of Quatford was granted to Roger de Montgomery, 1st Earl of Shrewsbury, by William the Conqueror. But it wasn't until Roger's son, Robert de Belleme, the 3rd Earl, transferred church and borough to Bridgnorth, which he saw as a much more defendable site. Robert's support of Robert Curthose's rebellion brought his attainder after his castle was besieged for three months by King Henry I in 1102, resulting in the town becoming a Royal Borough.

**Newport:** The market town of Newport was founded by the Normans (who called it *Novo Burgo*) near the old Roman road the Via Devana, which ran from Chester to Colchester, and between already established settlements at Plesc and Edgmond. The site chosen was a sandstone ridge to the west of Aqualate Mere, a natural lake, the largest in the Midlands, formed by melting glaciers; the River Meese flows from here to the River Tern. The lake and its abundant fisheries are mentioned in Domesday Book. Over time, the name changed from Nova Burgo to Newborough and finally to Newport.

**Ludlow:** The market town of Ludlow is famous for its royal castle, which sits on a promontory high above the River Teme. A place of old streets and quaint buildings, this medieval walled town is the largest town in the south-west of the county, with approaching 500 listed medieval and Tudor-style half-timbered buildings. The name Ludlow derives from the Old English 'Hlud-Hluw', which morphed into Lodelowe; 'Hlud' means loud waters, and 'Hlaw' means hill. In Welsh it's Llwydlo. A thirteenth-century poem mentions that for a long time Ludlow was called Dinham.

**Market Drayton (Draitune):** A small market town, Market Drayton was known previously as Drayton in Hales, and before that as Drayton. Market Drayton claims to be the home of gingerbread.

**Whitchurch (Westune/Westone):** Another market town, Whitchurch is the oldest continuously inhabited town in the county, having originally been settled by the Romans some time between AD 52 and 70. In those far-off days Whitchurch was called Mediolanum (a name shared with Milan), which means 'place in the middle of a plain'. The town's current name derives from the Norman period, during which it housed a church built of white stone: White church. Sadly, that original church is gone; its replacement was built in 1712 of red sandstone.

**Shifnal (Iteshale):** The market town of Shifnal may originate from Roman times, but as seventh-century Idsall it was probably founded in the days of the Angles. In the ninth century the town is believed to have been known as 'Scuffanhalch', 'Scuffa' being the name of a person, and 'halh' meaning valley. Over the centuries, the town has been known as 'Idsall' and 'Shifnal', swapping between the two. A ninth-century charter refers to 'Iddeshale', which means 'Idi's nook or corner'. The village is mentioned in Domesday Book, which records that 'Robert, son of Theobald, holds of Earl Roger Itesdale' and was lost by Saxon Earl Morcar when he rebelled against the Norman invaders. The Wesley Brook, a tributary of the River Worfe, runs through the town. There are claims that Idsall means 'Hall of Ide', and that Shifnal means 'Hall of Sceafa'.

**Wem (Weme):** Yet another market town, Wem's name derives from the Saxon word 'wamm', meaning marsh, and is believed to have been settled by the Celtic Iron Age tribe the Cornovii before the Roman conquest. The town is reported in Domesday Book as consisting of four manors. Wem is the birthplace of the Eckford Sweet Pea, named after Henry Eckford, the nurseryman who first cultivated the plant. The town is also famous for Wem Ales, and has been a site of beer brewing certainly since as early as 1700.

# A FEW OF THE ODD PLACE NAMES TO BE FOUND IN SHROPSHIRE

- Chemistry, near Whitchurch
- Loggerheads, near Shrewsbury
- The Bog, south-west of Shrewsbury
- The Four Alls, near Market Drayton
- Sweet Appletree, near Market Drayton
- Wig Wig, near Much Wenlock
- Homer, near Much Wenlock
- Titterstone Clee, one of the three Clee hills
- Ruyton-XI-Towns, north-west of Shrewsbury
- Snailbeach, south-west of Shrewsbury

Here are a few more that are, let's say, a bit different:

- The Coats, near Longville-in-the-Dale
- The Fegg, also near Longville-in-the-Dale
- Overs, near Bridges
- Catstree, near Bridgnorth
- Ale Oak, in south-west Shropshire
- Cabin, near Bishop's Castle
- The Sheet, near Ludlow

- Hook-a-Gate, near Shrewsbury
- Diddlebury, near Craven Arms
- Betton Strange, near Shrewsbury
- Tong, near Albrighton
- Cockshutt, near Wem
- Howle, north of Telford
- Long Waste, north of Telford
- Willey, near Broseley
- Badger, near Bridgnorth
- Pant, near Oswestry
- Grimpo, near Oswestry
- Gobowen, near Oswestry
- Knockin, near Oswestry
- Yockleton, near Shrewsbury
- Pulley, near Shrewsbury
- Crowsnest, near Shrewsbury
- Hope, near Shrewsbury
- Wagbeach, near Shrewsbury
- Nox, near Shrewsbury
- Shelve, near Shrewsbury
- Cross Houses, near Shrewsbury
- Cruckmeole, near Shrewsbury
- Hungry Hatton, near Market Drayton
- Lower Down, near Bishops Castle
- Sheets, near Shrewsbury
- Shit Brook, a small culverted stream in Much Wenlock

And lastly, a couple of oddly named streets:

- Grope Lane, Shrewsbury
- Gullet Passage, Shrewsbury
- Dog In The Lane, Telford
- Tarts Hill Lane, Whitchurch

There are many more odd names – if you look hard enough, you'll find them.

Moving from the semi-ridiculous to the sublime, now for a few of the county's most noteworthy places.

GROPE LANE
SHREWSBURY

# SHROPSHIRE'S UNESCO
# WORLD HERITAGE SITES

**The Ironbridge Gorge World Heritage Site:** In terms of the Industrial Revolution, the Ironbridge Gorge is one of the most important places in the world. It all began in 1709, when a man named Abraham Darby I (1678–1717) (see People), pioneered the use of coke instead of charcoal to smelt iron ore, making the process much more economic. For almost two centuries the Gorge prospered through three generations of Darbys, until a decline in industry in the 1900s sped the end of the Gorge as a major industrial force.

THE IRONBRIDGE

On a happier note, the Gorge's industrial archaeology has been the subject of an extensive restoration programme, enabling today's and future generations to experience the exciting complex of ten living museums, at the heart of which is the world-famous bridge that gave its name to the town – Ironbridge.

Pausing on and beside the spectacular and beautiful Ironbridge spanning the River Severn just the other day, I was beguiled by the sweeping arc of the main structure and the intricate supports, which have delighted the eye of so many for over 200 years. Sir Nikolaus Pevsner, the noted scholar of art and architecture describes the structure thus: 'The earliest bridge of cold blast iron designed by Abraham Darby in 1778. The charm as well as the admirable boldness of the bridge is indeed its light and lacy thinness.' Pevsner is wrong in attributing the design of the bridge to Mr Darby. The iron used in the construction was indeed smelted and cast in his furnaces and workshops, but the original designer was Shrewsbury architect Thomas Farnolls Pritchard (1723–77). A modified version of his design was used and work started in 1777, but sadly Pritchard died before the bridge was completed. The bridge itself was originally to be a timber construction, but Abraham Darby III and Ironmaster John Wilkinson demanded that it be made of iron. The full story of how the iron bridge came to be built gives a fascinating view of eighteenth-century business. The bridge was opened in 1779. (For more details, I recommend the website of the Broseley Local History Society.)

Coalbrookdale and Ironbridge are rightly regarded as the birthplace of the Industrial Revolution. The Ironbridge Gorge is now a designated UNESCO World Heritage Site, putting it in the exalted company of the Taj Mahal, the Pyramids, the Great Wall of China, and the Grand Canyon, among others. But of course we have two World Heritage Sites in Shropshire – the other is the Pontcysyllte Aqueduct and Canal.

**The Pontcysyllte Aqueduct and Canal:** This World Heritage Site sits on the border between Shropshire and Powys, and is most definitely the work of Thomas Telford, who built it between 1795 and 1805. The design, featuring a cast-iron trough surmounting eighteen stone piers, carries the Shropshire Union Canal 126ft above the River Dee. 'The river in the sky', as it has been fondly called, is 1,007ft long – a truly remarkable feat of engineering. The braver among us can take a breathtaking trip along the aqueduct on a canal boat, or you can just walk across. Whichever method of transport you choose, you will need a good head for heights.

Here are a few other noteworthy places in Shropshire:

**Chirk Aqueduct and Viaduct:** Another marvellous feat of engineering that was finished in 1801 and lies a few miles north of Pontcysyllte, the aqueduct carries the Llangollen branch of the Shropshire Union Canal far above the Ceiriog Valley. The 420m-long tunnel that sits adjacent to the aqueduct is known locally as 'The Darkie'.

**Hawkstone Park and Follies:** This wonderfully romantic site near Weston-under-Redcastle holds many surprises: caves, and grottos decorated with shells, coral and stained glass, cliffs, the Red Castle, tales of hermits, of King Arthur and the Green Knight, all connected by a myriad of twisting trails that wind through rhododendrons and pine trees. Many famous people have been drawn here to see the wonders for themselves, among them Doctor Johnson, who wrote: 'Art has proceeded no further than to make the succession of wonders safely accessible.'

**Wroxeter Roman City:** Once the fourth-largest city in Roman Britain, Viroconium Cornoviorum began life as a legionary fortress and was later developed into a thriving civilian settlement with a population of around 6,000, many of them retired legionnaires and traders.

**Offa's Dyke:** One of two such ancient dykes running through Shropshire – the other is Wat's Dyke. Offa's Dyke is the longest archaeological monument in Britain, an impressive 177-mile long rampart and ditch-style earthwork roughly following the border between England and Wales, the ditch being on the Welsh side. It is thought that the ditch was originally around 27m wide, and the rampart about 8m tall from the bottom of the ditch. Although the exact origins of the dyke are shrouded in mystery, King Alfred's biographer, a chap named Asser, was the first to mention it: 'a certain vigorous king called Offa had a great dyke built between Wales and Mercia from sea to sea.'

Offa was King of Mercia from AD 757–796. His kingdom covered a large area of England, its northern boundary being somewhere between the River Trent and the Mersey, extending south to the

Thames Valley, and west from the Welsh border to the Fens in the east. At times Offa also controlled Kent, East Anglia and Lincoln. The dyke is believed to have been constructed around AD 785–790, and must have taken many years to complete. The original purpose was probably a fortified defensive barrier to keep out the marauding Welsh princes of Powys (Welsh-speaking Cymry – Welsh as the English called them), but it may simply have marked an agreed boundary.

**Wat's Dyke:** A 40-mile (64km) non-continuous earthwork running from Basingwerk on the River Dee estuary to Maesbrook in Shropshire. Wat was King of the South Saxons around AD 692, but it is now thought unlikely that the dyke was built in his time. Its origins have been the subject of many disputes. It was originally thought to date back to the eighth century, and to have been built by Æthelbald, King of Mercia from AD 716–757, but that in itself is unclear. It seems unlikely that the dyke's construction will ever be correctly dated. Like Offa's Dyke, the earthwork consists of a bank and ditch, with the ditch on the Welsh side.

# NATIONAL TRUST PROPERTIES IN SHROPSHIRE

**Attingham Park:** Attingham Park, at Atcham, derives its name from the Saxon 'dwelling of the people of Saint Eata'. Standing on the site of an earlier house called Tern Hall, itself named after the nearby River Tern, Attingham was built in 1785 for Noel Hill, the 1st Baron Berwick, who actually moved the London to Holyhead Road so that it would be further from the house. Not content with this, the medieval village of Berwick Maviston was also removed to improve the park. The motto of the family is: 'Let wealth be his who knows its use.'

The scandal of the family was the second Lord Berwick. He never married, preferring the company of his friend and agent, Francis Walford, for whom he built nearby Cronkhill. This delightful Italianate villa was designed by John Nash, the renowned Regency architect, who also designed London's Regent Street, and the Royal Pavilion at Brighton. The fifth Lord Berwick invented the innovative 'Cronkill rifle' and the eighth Lord Berwick was president of the RSPCA for twenty-five years.

**Benthall Hall:** This lovely sixteenth-century house near Broseley was built some time around 1535, most likely on the site of an earlier manor house. During the English Civil War the house was garrisoned for the king, and it was the scene of several skirmishes. Benthall Hall was taken over by the National Trust in 1958. The thirtieth generation of the Benthall family still occupies the property.

BENTHALL HALL

**Carding Mill Valley, Church Stretton:** Covering an area of 4,942 acres (2,000ha), this beautiful valley is one of Shropshire's most important areas for wildlife, geology, landscape and archaeology, flanked by picturesque heather-covered hills. The topmost hills reward the hearty climber with the most wonderful views, and on a clear day you can see for over 50 miles in every direction. The Mynd is also home to the Midland Gliding Club.

**Dudmaston Hall and Estate, Quatt, near Bridgnorth:** The estate came into the Wolryche/Wolryche-Whitmore family in 1403, when William Wolryche of Much Wenlock married its heiress, Margaret de Dudmaston. The current house was built over a period in the seventeenth and eighteenth centuries, replacing a much older medieval structure believed to have been a fortified manor house. The first baronet, Sir Thomas Wolryche (1598–1688) was a staunch supporter of King Charles I, who knighted him in July 1641, and bestowed the baronage upon him a few weeks later. He raised troops and served as governor of Bridgnorth Castle, garrisoning the castle for the king (see Castles and Fortifications, Bridgnorth Castle). Parliament subsequently fined him more than £730. Sir Thomas's fifth son, John, took control of Dudmaston in 1668, the eldest son, Francis, having being declared a lunatic. John began the construction of the core of the present elegant sandstone house, but died before it was completed. His son, Sir Thomas, the third baronet, and his descendants saw the project through. The fourth baronet, Sir John Wolryche, turned out to be a bit of a lad, gambling away large wads of cash. In 1723, on his way home after attending a horse race meeting at Chelmarsh, he decided to ford the River Severn and was drowned.

The nearby model village of Quatt, the work of London architect John Birch, has a number of charming cottages, built in 1870 for the workers and tenants of the Dudmaston estate.

Dudmaston Hall houses a unique collection of modern and contemporary art, plus a host of botanical drawings and watercolours bought by diplomat Sir George and Lady Rachel Labouchere. The gardens offer many woodland walks around its huge lake.

**Morville Hall, near Bridgnorth:** This fine Elizabethan house, originally built around 1546 and enlarged in the mid-1700s, stands on the site of the abandoned Morville Priory. The gardens incorporate the Dower House Gardens. The property has belonged to the National Trust since 1965.

**Sunnycroft:** This Victorian gentleman's residence in Wellington was built in 1880, and extended in 1899. It was bequeathed to the National Trust in 1997.

**Wilderhope Manor:** Longville-in-the-Dale, near Much Wenlock, the Elizabethan Wilderhope Manor is a fine limestone manor house built around 1585 for Francis Smallman, in whose family it stayed until 1734, when it was sold and left to deteriorate. The W.A. Cadbury Trust bought the property in 1936, on the condition that it be turned into a youth hostel. It is now managed by the National Trust and the stable block is a Grade II listed building. During the English Civil War, Wilderhope was owned by the Royalist Major Thomas Smallman, who was forced to flee on horseback to avoid capture by a troop of Parliamentary soldiers who gave chase. Major Smallman urged his horse down a steep slope on Wenlock Edge. Horse and rider plunged downwards, the major's fall being broken by an apple tree; sadly, the horse was killed. This spot on the Edge is now known as Major's Leap, where the ghosts of Major Smallman and his horse have been seen. They have also been seen at Wilderhope Manor.

# ENGLISH HERITAGE PROPERTIES IN SHROPSHIRE

**Acton Burnell Castle:** (see Castles)

**Cantlop Bridge:** Built in 1813, this 31ft long (9.5m) single-span cast-iron road bridge spans the Cound Brook, near Cross Houses. The structure may have been designed by Thomas Telford, as it reputedly bore an original plate inscribed 'Thomas Telford Esqr – Engineer – 1818', which has long since disappeared.

**Clun Castle:** (see Castles and Fortifications)

**Haughmond Abbey:** (see Abbeys and Churches)

**Iron Bridge:** (see Places)

**Langley Chapel:** Built in 1601, this Anglican chapel can be found near Acton Burnell.

**Mitchells Fold Stone Circle:** (see Stone Circles)

**Moreton Corbet Castle:** (see Castles and Fortifications)

**Old Oswestry Hill Fort:** (see Hill Forts)

**Stokesay Castle:** (see Castles and Fortifications)

**Wenlock Priory:** (see Abbeys and Churches)

**White Ladies Priory:** (see Abbeys and Churches)

**Wroxeter Roman City:** (see Places)

## STONE CIRCLES

**Mitchells Fold Stone Circle:** The legend of King Arthur is alive and kicking in Shropshire, and this ancient stone circle is very much part of the story. It is here that Arthur is thought to have become king by drawing the sword Excalibur from the stone. The Bronze Age circle of thirty stones (only fourteen remain), is believed to date from some time between 2000 and 1400 BC, and sits 1,083ft (330m) above sea level on dry heathland on Stapley Hill, a ridge high in the Shropshire Hills, near the village of White Grit. The fold is around 27m in diameter and the stones mostly less than 1m tall; the tallest stands at almost 2m. Thin ridges run alongside and through the circle, their purpose, if any, is not known. This fascinating Bronze Age stone circle, Shropshire's finest, is also called Medgel's Fold, or Madges Pinfold, and is to be found near Chirbury.

**Druid's Castle:** At Stapeley, not far from Mitchell's Fold, there once was a deserted cottage known locally as the Druid's Castle or Druid's Circle, near where three standing stones once stood, two of which survived well into the 1800s. One, leaning slightly, was about 1.2m x 1.2m x 10cm thick and faced south-east. When the stone was removed in 1878, a small three-handled earthenware vessel, long since lost, was said to have been discovered. It contained ashes and bits of leather. The second stone stood around 6m from the other, and was narrower. The cottage is now deserted and no traces of the stones can be found.

**Hoarstones:** Around 2.5km north-east of Mitchell's Fold, are the remains of the Hoarstone Stone Circle. Sometimes called the Henford, Marsh Pool or Black Marsh Circle. The name 'hoarstone' means boundary stone, and may come from being situated at the junction of three parish boundaries. The circle has a single stone of around 1m in height at its centre, surrounded by thirty-seven rough or undressed sarsen stones (silicified boulders of the kind found at Stonehenge), most of which are less than knee-high.

**Whetstones Circle:** Of this circle only fragments remain, having been largely dug up in the nineteenth century to build a boundary wall. Charcoal and bones were reportedly found under the stones.

## HILL FORTS

The county of Shropshire abounds with these wonderfully evocative sites.

**Oswestry Hill Fort:** Arthurian legend has it that this spectacularly mystical place is the birthplace of Ganhumara (Guinevere) (see The Legend of King Arthur), whose father, Ogyrfan, gave his name to the site: Caer Ogyrfan. The Iron Age fort comprises a series of seven banks and ditches, and is believed to have been the site for the Battle of Maes Cogwy in 642. This was when the Powys king Cynddylan of Pergwern, said to be the last descendant of King Arthur to rule in Shropshire, joined Penda, King of Mercia, to defeat King Oswald of Northumbria. Excavations show that the site was inhabited earlier, possibly during the Bronze Age. The habitable area on top of the hill covers approximately 6ha.

The county has many other ancient Iron Age hill forts, some scheduled, some unscheduled, such as those at Abdon Burf and Clee Burf on Brown Clee Hill; Bury Ditches on Sunnyhill, between Clun and Bishop's Castle; Bayston Hill (Burgs, and Bomere Wood) 3 miles south of Shrewsbury; Nordy Bank near Clee Saint Margaret, and Caer Caradoc. For a full, detailed list of hill forts, standing stones and menhirs, ring cairns and cairns, visit the Shropshire History website: www.shropshirehistory.com.

# 3

# ROYAL SHROPSHIRE

Shropshire has many connections with royalty. Here are a few:

**Henry III** concluded a peace treaty with Welsh leader, Prince Llewelyn, at Ludlow Castle. Henry and his queen, Eleanor of Castile, also visited Wenlock Priory on many occasions.

**Edward I** set up parliament in Shrewsbury in 1283, probably in the chapter house of the abbey.

**Richard III** also held a parliament in Shrewsbury, known as the 'Great Parliament'.

In 1485, **Henry, Earl of Richmond,** the future King Henry VII, stayed in a house in Wile Cop, Shrewsbury on his way to fight King Richard III at the Battle of Bosworth.

**Prince Arthur Tudor** (20 September 1486–2 April 1502), eldest son of King Henry VII, died at Ludlow Castle six months short of his sixteenth birthday. He and his new wife, Catherine of Aragon, contracted what was described as 'a malign vapour which proceeded from the air' (this may possibly be tuberculosis). Catherine recovered, but her teenage husband didn't. His heart is buried in a silver casket beneath the chancel of St Laurence's church, Ludlow. The rest of him is buried in Worcester Cathedral. Arthur's tragic death raised King Henry's second son, Henry (later Henry VIII) as heir to the throne.

The royal castle at Ludlow has housed many potential monarchs, including the young **Edward V and Richard of Shrewsbury**, Duke of

York, later to be known as the Princes in the Tower. Thanks to William Shakespeare, the story of the two young princes is well known, but before they met their untimely and mysterious deaths – or shall we say disappearance – Prince Edward and his younger brother Richard had spent most of their childhood years at Ludlow Castle. Prince Edward was there when he received the news of his father's death and he acceded to the title of Edward V. However, he was never crowned, for when he and his brother arrived in London they were lodged in the Tower. Their uncle, Richard, Duke of Gloucester, then became King Richard III, and although his guilt has never been proven, Shakespeare's play has settled the blame for their deaths firmly on Richard's shoulders.

When she was a young girl, the daughter of Catherine of Aragon and Henry VIII, **Princess Mary** (later Queen Mary I) spent three winters at Ludlow Castle. She stayed at Dogpole, the house of her mother's steward, John Rocke.

**Charles I** loved the Castle Walk in Bridgnorth so much that he is said to have called it 'his favourite walk in his entire kingdom'. When staying at the Council House in Shrewsbury, Charles I offered the burgesses of the town the chance to make their town a city – they refused. He may also have stayed at Chetwynd.

On 18 September 1642, **Charles I** raised his standard in the vicinity of Wellington (now part of Telford), and made the 'Wellington Declaration', also known as the 'Declaration of Wellington'. He addressed his assembled troops two days later on 20 September, declaring he would 'Uphold the Protestant Religion, the laws of England, and the Liberty of Parliament' – a statement so important that it was stamped on silver 10s. and silver half-crowns. The king's cousin, Prince Rupert of the Rhine, stayed in Shrewsbury and Bridgnorth.

Escaping after the Battle of Worcester in September 1651, the defeated **Charles Stuart** (crowned Charles II two years earlier in Scotland) travelled north, staying at Whiteladies Priory and Boscobel Hall, the home of the Penderel family. When Roundhead soldiers arrived to search the building, Charles famously took refuge in an oak tree in the grounds of the house. The estranged Scottish king was later taken across the Shropshire border to Moseley Old Hall (now National Trust). He also took shelter at Ashfield Hall, near Much Wenlock.

In 1687, **James II** visited Shrewsbury.

**George, Prince of Wales** (later George IV) stayed at Alderbury and at Loton Park.

In 1832, the 13-year-old **Princess Victoria** (later Queen Victoria) and her mother, the Duchess of Kent, slept in a room at Pitchford Hall, near Shrewsbury. She wrote in her diary that: 'It is a very comfortable yet curious looking house, striped black and white in the shape of a cottage.' She doesn't say whether she was amused! Princess Victoria opened the Royal Victoria Hotel in Newport in 1832.

Wartime Prime Minister Winston Churchill had secretly set aside Pitchford Hall for **King George VI, Queen Elizabeth** and the two princesses, Elizabeth and Margaret, as a rural refuge should Britain be invaded by Germany.

In July 2003, Ludlow Castle proudly welcomed **Elizabeth II** and the Duke of Edinburgh on the first visit of a reigning British monarch to the castle for many hundreds of years.

**Princes William and Harry** both trained at the Defence Helicopter Flying School based at RAF Shawbury. Prince William also spent time at RAF Cosford.

Royal visits to the county to open new buildings and suchlike are far too numerous to list.

## A COUPLE OF QUIRKY ROYAL
## CONNECTIONS WITH SHROPSHIRE

In 1931, Shropshire-born Anthony William Hall (1898–1947) claimed to be the direct descendant of King Henry VIII and Anne Boleyn through the male line, albeit that the birth of Hall's ancestor was prior to their actual marriage (i.e. the direct male line of King Henry VIII's illegitimate son). Hall, a police inspector in Shropshire, thus attempted to claim the throne of England. He wrote an open letter to the then king, George V, setting out his claim in detail. Hall also made many speeches, including one in Birmingham, in which he set out his credentials. He also challenged the king to a duel, the loser to be beheaded. Arrested many times for using 'scandalous language', Hall was arraigned in court, fined and bound over to keep the peace. Anthony Hall's claim was used as the basis for the 1999 novel *Heir Unapparent* by John Harrison.

Another Shropshire connection with King Henry VIII is a woman by the name of Elizabeth Blount, of Kinlet. Born some time between 1498 and 1502, Bessie Blount, as she was commonly known during her lifetime, was a mistress of the king. Bessie's father was Sir John Blount of Kinlet; her mother was Catherine Blount, née Pershall. Loyal servant Sir John Blount had accompanied King Henry to France in 1513 during the war against the French. Bessie Blount was a reputed beauty, nine or so years younger than the king, and first travelled to court as maid-of-honour to Queen Catherine of Aragon. The teenager caught Henry's roving eye, becoming his mistress some time around 1514–1515, for around eight years. Unfortunately, there is no known portrait of Elizabeth in existence, so we can only guess at what so attracted Henry. She died around 1549–1550.

# 4

# SHROPSHIRE FIRST AND LAST

## FIRST

The first iron bridge was built in Shropshire, and opened on 1 January 1781. The town that grew around it took the name Ironbridge.

The world's first iron boat was built and launched at Coalbrookdale in Shropshire in 1787. Ironmaster John Wilkinson (1728–1808), manufacturer of cannons, mortars and shells, thus solved his transport problems.

The world's first skyscraper was Ditherington Flax Mill in Shrewsbury, completed in 1797 at an estimated cost of £17,000, including the mill equipment. The architect was Derby-born Charles Wooley Bage (1751–1822).

The first university in Britain dedicated to agri-food science is Harper Adams University College in Edgmond, near Newport.

The first stagecoach service between London and Shrewsbury was running regularly in 1681.

On 6 September 1785, the first Irish Mail coach from London to Holyhead passed through Shrewsbury, causing so much excitement that many thousands turned out to see the coach arrive at Shrewsbury's Lion Hotel.

The first mail coach to Shrewsbury was established by Robert Lawrence, proprietor for many years of the Raven and Lion inns in the town.

The first ever footballer to win 100 caps was Ironbridge-born Billy Wright.

Telford United played in the first non-league FA Challenge Trophy Cup Final at Wembley in May 1971. I was there; they lost 2–0 to Macclesfield Town. They won it the following year.

Dawley-born Captain Matthew Webb was the first man to swim the English Channel.

Shropshire's Sir Gordon Richards was the first jockey to be knighted (see Sporting Shropshire).

# LAST

The Last Inn in Shropshire – no, don't worry, it's the name of a pub – is in the hamlet of Hengoed, near Oswestry.

The last use of stocks in Shrewsbury was in 1850, to secure a policeman convicted of being drunk and disorderly. Rumour has it that when he completed his sentence, he received a standing ovation from the crowd that had gathered, who even took up a collection for him.

The last recorded use of a brank (scold's bridle) in Shrewsbury was in 1846. A Frankwell woman was fitted with one for being rude to her neighbours.

The last woman to be publicly executed in Shropshire was Ann Harris, on 16 August 1828 (see Shropshire Murders).

The last man hanged at Shrewsbury was 21-year-old George Riley of Copthorne, who was executed by Albert Pierrepoint on 9 February 1961 for the murder of widow Adeline Mary Smith, aged 62.

# 5

# THE SIZE
# DEBATE

## LARGEST

Landlocked Shropshire is Britain's largest inland county at 1,346 square miles (3,487 sq km), including Telford and Wrekin. Wiltshire (including Swindon) is a smidge smaller at 1,345 square miles (3,485 sq km). (Figures are mid-estimates for 2011 from the Office of National Statistics.)

## LONGEST

The longest river in Britain is the River Severn (see Water and Waterways) at 220 miles (355km). Its longest stretch passes through Shropshire.

The longest canal in Shropshire is the 67-mile (108km) Shropshire Union Canal (see Water and Waterways).

## TALLEST/HIGHEST

The tallest hill in Shropshire is the Brown Clee Hill (Abdon Burf) at 1,791ft (546m) – often recorded as 1,772ft (540m). Second highest is Stiperstones (Manston Rock) at 1,759ft (536m). Third is Titterstone Clee Hill at 1,748ft (533m). The rest of the top ten are: 4. Long Mynd (Pole Bank) at 1,693ft (516m); 5. Brown Clee Hill (Clee Burf) at 1,673ft (510m); 6. Caer Caradoc Hill at 1,506ft (459m); 7. Heath Mynd at 1,502ft (458m); 8. The Wrekin at 1,335ft (407m); 9. Ragleth Hill at 1,306ft (398m); and at 10. Sunnyhill at 1,289ft (393m).

The tallest building in the county is a chimney at Ironbridge Power Station, at 673ft (205m). However, with the impending decommissioning of the station, this honour will have to change hands.

The world's tallest Doric column, at 133ft 6in (41m), supports the statue of Lord Rowland Hill in Shrewsbury.

The tallest man in Shropshire, known as 'the Shropshire Giant', was Thomas Dutton, born in Stoke-on-Tern in 1853. He was 7ft 3in, and weighed in at 23 stones. With his wife Betsy, Dutton toured throughout Britain and Europe with a travelling circus where he was billed as 'the British Soldier Giant'.

The tallest town crier in the world must surely be Shrewsbury's 7ft 2in gentle giant, Martin Wood. (I heartily recommend Martin's book *Crime and Punishment: Shrewsbury*, plus his ghost book, *Haunted Shrewsbury*.)

## LOWEST

The lowest ever temperature in England and Wales was recorded on 10 January 1982 at Harper Adams University in Edgmond Village, near Newport, at minus 26.1°C. Next day it was a mere minus 11.3°C.

## HEAVIEST

Also nicknamed the 'Shropshire Giant', William Ball (1795–1852) of Horsehay, Great Dawley weighed more than 40 stone despite being only 5ft 9in tall. From the tender age of 8, Ball was employed for forty years as a puddler and shingler at the Coalbrookdale Company's Horsehay Ironworks. He exhibited himself at county fairs and the Great Exhibition of 1851 as the largest man in Britain under the pseudonym 'John Bull'.

WILLIAM BALL "JOHN BULL"

# OLDEST

The oldest continuously inhabited town in Shropshire is Whitchurch, founded by the Romans as Mediolanum around AD 70.

The oldest timber-framed church in Shropshire is reputedly St Peter's in Melverley, Oswestry, built in 1401 to replace the timber-framed church burnt by Owain Glyn Dwr.

The world's oldest maker of tower clocks is believed to be J.B. Joyce and Company of Whitchurch, founded in 1690 by William Joyce in Cockshutt, north Shropshire. Their clocks are to be found all over the world, in such diverse places as Australia, China, and India. The company were involved in the manufacture of the clock at the Houses of Parliament, the great bell of which is Big Ben.

The claimant of the title 'oldest man in England' is surely (written with tongue firmly in cheek!) agricultural labourer Thomas Parr, nicknamed Old Parr, born in Winnington, near Alderbury, in 1483. He reputedly died aged 152 years and nine months old, having lived through the reigns of ten monarchs: Edward IV, Edward V, Richard III, Henry VII, Henry VIII, Queen Mary, Queen Elizabeth I, James I and Charles I. In 1635 he was taken to London, where he was presented to King Charles I. He died that same year, on 15 November, and was buried in Westminster Abbey. Some say it was the rich food and attention that killed him. His two grandsons are said to have lived to the age of 127, and his great-grandson a mere 124.

It is worth mentioning a few other centenarians: William Wakley, born around 1590 in Shifnal, died aged 124, and was buried at Adbaston in 1714. Mary Yates died at 127 and was reputed to have walked from Shifnal to London in 1660 when she was 17. Elsie Day (née Merrington) (1885–1996), another native of Dawley, died aged 110 years and nine months. It makes you wonder if the years were shorter in those days.

The Three Tuns public house in Bishop's Castle claims to be the oldest working brewery in Britain, having brewed beer there since 1642, when their first licence was granted.

The oldest theme park is surely Hawkstone Park and Follies, which dates back to before the eighteenth century.

The world's oldest surviving iron aqueduct is at Longdon-on-Tern, north-east of Shrewsbury, which opened in 1797.

The honour of being the oldest inn in the county is certainly a subject that could start a healthy, or heated, debate over a pint or three. First we have to establish the answer to this question: is an inn the same as a pub? Make your own mind up. Here are a few contenders to consider:

The Three Horseshoes in Alveley near Bridgnorth claims to be Shropshire's oldest public house. The date 1406 is proudly painted on the side of the pub.

The Swan Inn at Aston Munslow near Much Wenlock, established in 1350, claims the title of Shropshire's oldest inn. Legend has it that the Swan was once a fourteenth-century coaching inn and once accommodated the infamous highwayman Dick Turpin.

The Royal Oak at Cardington near Church Stretton claims to be the oldest continually licensed pub in Shropshire, since some time in the fifteenth century. There are claims that there was a drinking establishment here in the eleventh century. Cardintune itself is certainly mentioned in Domesday Book.

Ellesmere has a couple of oldies: the White Hart, a fine black-and-white timber-framed Grade II listed building, built in the seventeenth century, and the Red Lion, a lovely sixteenth-century coaching inn.

The Bull Hotel in Ludlow, another Grade II listed building, dates back to 1199, when it was believed to have been built to house the workmen who built St Laurence's church. Of course, in those days it wasn't a place for drinking.

The Old Three Pigeons in Nesscliffe, the haunt of highwayman Sir Humphrey Kynaston, has served the local community since 1405.

Established in 1875, Shrewsbury Flower
Show is the oldest in the world.

## STEEPEST

Connecting Bridgnorth's High Town and
Low Town is Britain's steepest funicular
railway, the Bridgnorth Cliff Railway, which has
been taking people up and down the 111ft vertical
sandstone cliffs for over a century. It was originally
powered by a water balance system, but now by an
electric winding engine. Construction of the track, 201ft long at an
incline of 33°, began on 2 November 1891 and it was opened on
7 July 1892.

# 6

# CRIME, PUNISHMENT AND THE POOR

Following the birth of the Industrial Revolution, the eighteenth and nineteenth centuries saw crime levels in Britain rise as people became more mobile, seeking work away from more traditional occupations in agriculture, and, of course, the population of towns increased steadily. At the turn of the nineteenth century the population of the country was around 16 million; by 1900 the population was approaching 42 million. Obviously more people means more crime, and during this period policing became a much more serious requirement, as did the resulting punishment.

The infamous 'Bloody Code' saw people severely punished for all manner of crimes that we might call petty today. In the nineteenth century more than 200 types of crime carried the death penalty. Though in practice most were commuted to a less severe punishment, people committing any kind of a felony in the eighteenth century and the early 1800s might find themselves on the wrong end of the hangman's rope. Murder, rape, sodomy, animal theft (horses, sheep and cows in particular), highway robbery, stabbing, housebreaking, theft, rioting, killing a cow, burglary, private theft, sacrilege, stealing from a wreck, forgery, abetting murder and arson – all and more were punishable by death. During the century over 3,500 people were hanged in England and Wales alone; of these only 1,353 were executed for the crime of murder.

For a few years, transportation to the colonies, such as Australia and the like, was deemed an effective solution for crimes less serious than murder – on the 'out of sight, out of mind' principle. Few of these convicts ever returned to Britain. The 1850s brought a change in attitude, and the death penalty now applied only to murder and treason. The penalty of transportation came to an end in 1867.

Of course, not everyone turned to crime to support their family and the destitute and other unfortunates were placed in workhouses. The Poor Law Unions in Shropshire were at Atcham, Bridgnorth, Church Stretton, Cleobury Mortimer, Clun, Ellesmere, Ludlow, Madeley, Market Drayton, Newport, Oswestry, Shifnal, Wellington, Wem and Whitchurch.

In a 1901 survey of Shropshire, it was noted that the number of pauper inmates of workhouse establishments in the Registration County was 1,808 persons of all ages. Of this number, 1,410 were male and 668 female. Many of these inmates were at an advanced age.

The same survey provided other fascinating statistics:

There were eighty prisoners in Shrewsbury Prison: seventy-five male and five female.

In the whole of Shropshire, 204 people were blind, three of these also suffered some other infirmity; 112 were deaf and dumb, three of these also suffering some other infirmity; and nine were dumb, but not deaf.

The number of 'lunatics' was a staggering 856, plus 376 classed as 'imbeciles and being of feeble-mind', including six who were 'otherwise afflicted'. Of this total of 1,232, there were 989 inmates of various institutions, including 868 in public and private psychiatric hospitals, 121 classed as 'imbeciles' or of 'feeble-mind' in workhouses. The remaining 243 resided with relatives or in unlicensed houses, of whom five were stated as being 'lunatics', and the rest as being either 'imbeciles' or of 'feeble-mind'.

Situated near the railway station, near the site of the medieval prison, Dana Gaol, Her Majesty's Prison in Shrewsbury, closed in March 2013. There had been a prison on the site since 1793, but the present building was constructed in 1877. It had ceased to take female convicts after 1922.

Shropshire has seen its fair share of executions. They were originally carried out in public as a deterrent to would-be criminals, more often at the place where the crime had been committed. However, this was not always the case in Shropshire. Executions in Shrewsbury were carried out either at Old Heath or in front of Shrewsbury Prison. Executions drew large crowds, which attracted petty criminals, specifically pickpockets, thus increasing the incidence of crime rather than deterring it. The Capital Punishment within Prisons Act of 1868 brought this practice to an end, and subsequent executions took place behind closed doors within the county prison. Before the Act, a lot of people made money from these spectacles, renting rooms overlooking the gallows and selling 'Penny Dreadfuls' – pamphlets with an over-dramatised account of the condemned's crime.

Between 1787 and 1793, twenty-six people were executed on the gallows at Old Heath. The last four were John Mumford, Richard Simister, William Richards and Daniel Sheldon (alias Whiley) – all for the burglary of the shop of John Jackson, mercer, of Halesowen.

From 1735 to 1800, there were 114 executions in Shropshire, and from 1800 to 1961, sixty-four men and eight women were executed at Shrewsbury.

In 1735, a man by the name of John Wayne was executed by hanging for the crime of horse stealing.

On Tuesday, 21 April 1767, John Scott was executed at Bridgnorth for housebreaking. His body was hanged in chains there afterwards.

In 1818, John Richards stole eight nice fat sheep from local farmer John Wilson. Richards was in bed with his new wife of five days when he was arrested. At his trial he was found guilty and was executed at Shrewsbury at around midday in the presence of a huge crowd.

Prior to the 1850s, the favoured method of hanging was known as the 'short drop'. This method relied on the condemned person's body weight and it often took some time for death to occur. More affluent victims often paid the hangman to tug on their feet to speed up their death – slow strangulation could take fifteen minutes. In 1874, the powers that be decided that hanging should be more compassionate, and the 'long drop' method was introduced, where the condemned's neck was snapped – more humane, but still resulting in death. Now it was necessary to make a calculation to determine the correct length of rope relative to their weight (i.e. heavier convicts need a shorter rope, lighter individuals a longer rope) for a rapid death. Following execution, some bodies were buried and some were cut up in the name of medical science. The 1752 Murder Act made the latter compulsory until 1834.

Popular punishments for petty crimes included the stocks, pillory and the whipping post. Some criminals were actively encouraged to join the army or navy. Sticking someone in the stocks also meant they didn't have to be housed in a jail and provided great entertainment for the locals, who could chuck rotten vegetables

(and other disgusting stuff), and hurl abuse at
those locked in them. Stocks secured the legs
of sitting offenders, whereas the pillory forced
the offender to stand with his head and arms
secured, a practice that ceased in 1837.

Flogging or whipping in public as an example to
others continued well into the 1800s. This practice
was superseded by public birching. Apparently,
in 1801, a Much Wenlock man, Edward
Browne, was tied to the back of a cart and
dragged around the town for two hours, being
whipped all the way.

Other punishments
included the brank
(sometimes called a
Scold's Bridle), an
iron-framed helmet
with a sharp metal
gag to hold the tongue
plate. It was used to punish
gossips, disturbers of
the peace, and anyone
convicted of noisy and
abusive behaviour;
the guilty was often
led around the
town to deter others
from such behaviour.

Don't let us forget the old ducking stool, once very popular in
Britain prior to the 1800s. Its use was the same as with the brank –
for gossips and rumour-spreaders.

The *Shrewsbury Chronicle* of 16 August 1793 reported that
Shrewsbury's new prison at Howard's Bank cost around £30,000.
The original prison was in the grounds of Shrewsbury Castle. In 1536,
the sheriff applied to have the gaol moved from the dilapidated

prison near the town's library; it was built fifty years later and known as the Sheriff's Gaol. It was pulled down in 1704, and a new prison built.

Prior to 1800, there wasn't much in the way of organised policing; most towns did their own thing, with elected constables more likely to be hated than appreciated. Two Acts of Parliament changed all that: the Municipal Corporation Act of 1835, and the Rural Constabulary Act of 1839. These Acts allowed the establishment of a permanent police force and by 1856 every county was compulsorily obliged to create one, which was controlled by local councillors and magistrates. This led to the foundation of borough police forces throughout Shropshire.

## POLICE

Bridgnorth's police force was established in 1836, and by 1880 consisted of a chief constable, a sergeant and three constables. Before this there were amateur parish constables.

These borough police forces were augmented by a rural police force, which was established to police the countryside. It was known as the Shropshire Constabulary, a force of six divisions, each responsible for a specific section of the county. By 1879 the Constabulary comprised almost 200 men; ten years later it had increased to 350 officers.

The Shropshire county police force was further divided in 1887, to oversee the towns of Shrewsbury, Oswestry, Whitchurch, Wellington, Bridgnorth, Church Stretton,

Pontesbury and Burford, each controlled by a Superintendent of Police. An Act of Parliament was passed in 1888, abolishing borough police forces in favour of a more organised approach to policing.

Separate from Shropshire's formal police forces there were other privately funded groups of crimefighters, such as the Newport Association for the Prosecution of Felons. These organisations mainly dealt with petty crime and acts of vandalism, offering money for information leading to arrests, and funding the prosecution of offenders in court. There were a few other such associations in the county.

# 7

# SHROPSHIRE RIOTS

In Shropshire and in towns around the country, 1715 saw a series of riots in protest against the choice of George Ludwig, Elector of Hanover as the next king of England, following the death of Queen Anne the previous year, the last of England's Stuart monarchs. The riots were timed and organised to coincide with George I's birthday on 28 May, and on the following day, which was the anniversary of the restoration of the monarchy that had brought King Charles II to the throne. Other riots took place on 10 June, the birthday of James Francis Edward Stuart – 'the Old Pretender' (son of King James II).

King George I had dismissed the Tories from office in favour of a majority, and unpopular, Whig government. His coronation in October 1715 caused rioting in more than twenty English towns. Around 2,000 protestors took part in the riots in Shropshire, Staffordshire and Worcestershire, hundreds in Birmingham, and around 500 people were arrested for felonious rioting. The Whig government responded by passing the infamous Riot Act, which gave powers to magistrates and justices of the peace to take legal action to break up riotous assembly. On these symbolic dates, rioters deliberately attacked dissenting chapels allied to the new king and the Whig party. In Lancashire and the West Midlands more than thirty dissenting chapels were attacked.

The following paper was posted in Shrewsbury during the riots:

We Gentlemen of the Loyal Mob of *Shrewsbury*, do issue out this Proclamation to all Dissenters from the Church of *England*, of what Kind or Denomination soever, whether Independent, Baptists or Quakers: If you, or any of you, do encourage or suffer any of that damnable Faction called Presbyterians, to assemble themselves amongst you, in any of your Conventicles, at the time of Divine Worship, you may expect to meet with the same that they have been treated with. Given under our Hands and Seals the 11th Day of July 1715. *God save the King.*

The Hanoverian George I had come to the throne in accordance with the 1701 Act of Settlement, thus excluding the rightful Stuart king, James Francis Edward Stuart, Queen Anne's half-brother.

The general election held in 1715, which resulted in a Whig majority, also saw a number of riots, with the Tories proscripted from office. A number of ex-Tory ministers found themselves impeached by the new government.

Shropshire's pivotal role in the Industrial Revolution, and the immense social changes it brought to the lives of the county's working men, was inevitably accompanied by a degree of dissatisfaction and conflict. The development of industry, iron, coal, ceramics and glass in the county saw harsh working conditions, often accompanied by poor wages, forcing disgruntled individuals to band together in collective protest, which resulted in a spate of riotous assemblies. To combat this growing unrest, Parliament passed dozens of Acts designed to outlaw trade unions in specifically targeted industries, until finally the 1799/1800 Combination Acts were passed to cover every industry.

In the eighteenth century, food riots brought people together in protest at the high price of bread, the staple diet of the masses. The cause? The exorbitant price of wheat. In 1756, Broseley miners rioted in Much Wenlock in an attempt to force bakers to sell bread at a fair and affordable price, and severe reprisals were threatened. Ten years later an angry mob of Clee Hill colliers gathered in Ludlow, destroying a building used for distilling alcohol from wheat.

The Battle of Cinderloo: This took place on 1 February 1821, when a group of Dawley colliers went on strike. This was a time when trade unionism had been officially outlawed under the Combination Acts. The miners' grievance stemmed from the mine owners' attempt in June of the previous year (1820) to reduce wages – by 6*d* a day from an average wage of 15*s* a week – who blamed the falling price of iron as the cause. The 1820 strike developed into violent clashes when the Shropshire Yeomanry were called out to protect property. It was soon quelled, resulting in few injuries, and no action to reduce wages.

The same trouble reared its head again when the owners made a second attempt at lowering wages. It came to a head on 1 February 1821, when colliers from the east Shropshire coalfields once again went on strike, damaging pithead equipment and, supported by local iron workers, effectively stopped production. Next day, a mob of striking colliers marched from Donnington Wood, damaging furnaces at a number of ironworks, at Old Park, Lightmoor, Dawley Castle and Horsehay. The mob's next planned stop was to be Coalbrookdale, but instead the colliers decided to retrace their steps. By 3 p.m. the mob had swelled to over 4,000 men, women and children. The Shropshire Yeomanry and Special Constables were called out by the owners, and the two opposing factions met close to Cinder Hills, two industrial spoil heaps, near the ironworks at Old Park. The Riot Act was read out by Thomas Eyton, one of the magistrates accompanying the soldiers, but the colliers started to throw missiles at them. Lieutenant Colonel William Cludde, in command of the detachment of Yeoman cavalry, ordered his troops to advance, and peace officers to seize the ringleaders. Two rioters were arrested by constables. When the pelting continued, Cludde then ordered his men to open fire on the crowd, killing one of the strikers, 18-year-old William Bird, and mortally wounding Thomas Gittins. Thomas Palin was also wounded, as were several others. The stunned crowd lost heart and dispersed. Nine men were taken by the soldiers.

At the Salop Assizes on 25 March 1821, two of the miners, Thomas Palin and Samuel Hayward, subsequently received the death sentence, and despite appeals for clemency by the owners, Thomas Palin was hanged. Samuel Hayward was reprieved, serving nine months of hard labour.

Ironically, all the riot achieved was damage to plants at the pit and ironworks, which in turn caused a loss of jobs. Many families were subsequently left destitute. And, of course, the employers forced through the wage cuts that were at the heart of the dispute, albeit some were less severe than others.

Less than two years earlier, the Peterloo massacre in Manchester had seen a similar riot suppressed in a most bloody way by the sabre-wielding cavalry. Peterloo was so named in ironic reference to the Battle of Waterloo in 1815. The Battle of Cinderloo continued that theme.

Trade unions in the mining industry grew out of such action to guard against reduction in wages, or changes to working conditions, plus the high cost of food, particularly bread. The following decades saw a repeat of this burgeoning unrest between workers and employers, culminating in the General Strike of 1842, against the backcloth of the Chartist movement's demand for parliamentary reform.

The 'Swing' Riots of 1830 and 1831 were caused by the same age-old problems: poor wages and working conditions, and high food prices. Three or four bad winters coupled with the development of new-fangled agricultural machinery, particularly the threshing machine, severely restricted agricultural labourers' chances of obtaining employment during the winter. The threshing machine therefore became the symbolic target for rioters.

In February 1830, the first threatening letter was received, the start of a flurry of letters called 'Swing letters' because many were signed by the mythical Captain Swing. So called 'Swing letters' were sent to farmers and factory owners containing threats to machinery and property, demanding higher wages and the removal of labour-saving machinery. In the autumn of 1830, agricultural workers, mostly in the south of England, banded together in an attempt to improve their quality of life. However, by early 1831, many of the protesters had been arrested, making it even harder for families who had suffered the jailing of their main breadwinner, or awaited transportation to Australia or Van Diemen's Land (Tasmania).

Riots spread west and north after the destruction of a threshing machine in Kent in August 1830, and a number of Shropshire men – along with rioters from Bedfordshire, Cambridgeshire, Derbyshire, Herefordshire, Hertfordshire, Somerset and Staffordshire – were transported. However, the counties with the highest number of transportees were Berkshire, Buckinghamshire, Dorset, Essex, Gloucestershire, Hampshire, Huntingdonshire, Kent, Norfolk, Oxfordshire, Suffolk, Sussex and Wiltshire. Haystacks and barns were burned, and workhouses and their officers attacked. Other attacks were made on wrought iron foundries, and rioters destroyed machinery in Kidderminster and Redditch.

When Lord Melbourne took office as home secretary in November 1830, county yeomanry were mobilised and special constables sworn in, supplemented by gangs of riotbusters organised by landowners, and by the end of the year the rioting had almost been stamped out. Around 2,000 men and women had been arrested. A special commission to deal with the rioters was set up, and most were tried at assize courts or quarter sessions. But some riots and demonstrations continued into 1831, with increasing cases of arson and destruction of the evil threshing machine. Despite many petitions for leniency, in total nineteen men were executed, and over 600 sentenced to imprisonment. Around 500 were sentenced to transportation for either seven or fourteen years, or, in the most extreme cases, for life.

One of the oddest riots was in Market Drayton in September 1868, which lasted for two days. Here there was widespread opposition to the increasing number of private water closets following measures taken by the wealthier inhabitants of the town to improve the provision of sanitary facilities.

## THE SHREWSBURY PICKETS

Five months after the end of the twelve-week national builders strike in 1972, twenty-four picketers were arrested in connection with an incident at a McAlpine site in Shrewsbury on 6 September 1972. They were charged with a staggering 242 offences between them, including unlawful assembly, intimidation, assault, criminal damage and affray. They were tried at Shrewsbury Crown Court in 1973. Six received custodial sentences: Des Warren for three years, Eric (Ricky) Tomlinson (now an actor famous as Jim Royle in *The Royle Family* and for his role in *Brookside*) for two years and John McKinsie Jones for nine months. Warren and Tomlinson became known as the Shrewsbury Two. The campaign to clear their name still goes on.

# 8

# QUIRKY FACTS
# AND ODDITIES

## ARCHITECTURE

Towering over Shrewsbury at a height of 133ft 6in, Lord Hill's Doric-style column is the tallest of its kind in the world. The monument stands in the centre of a traffic island opposite Shire Hall, the headquarters of Shropshire County Council, a little way up the road from the hotel that bears the great man's name.

Cleobury Mortimer's twelfth-century St Mary's church has a twisted spire. The sixteenth-century octagonal wooden spire has twisted over time, its oak timbers warped due to damp-induced rot. The stone walls and pillars of the church also lean, having slipped out of shape. In 1794 Thomas Telford was called in to stabilise the building.

## GEOLOGY

The world's oldest recognised Lower Cambrian fossil, a Trilobite (*Callavia Callavei*), was discovered in 1888 in Comley Quarry at Caer Caradoc in Shropshire.

Shropshire is a magnet for geologists, particularly in the south of the county, where there are rocks from eleven of the planet's thirteen geological periods.

The towns of Ludlow and Wenlock Edge have given their names to geological periods.

## HISTORICAL AND WARTIME SHROPSHIRE

Shrewsbury was the first English town entered by Henry Tudor, Earl of Richmond (later Henry VII), and his Lancastrian army en route to do battle with King Richard III at Bosworth.

During the Peninsular War against Napoleon Bonaparte, French prisoners were billeted in Bishop's Castle.

The village of Whittington in north Shropshire is said to have been the home of the legendary Dick Whittington, who, with his equally famous cat, reputedly walked to London to seek fame and fortune. He went on to become Lord Mayor of London.

More than 255 men from the Bridgnorth area volunteered in the first months of the First World War, when Britain declared war on Germany on 4 August 1914. The number had swelled to over 400 by December 1914. Their names were published in the *Bridgnorth Journal* on 26 December 1914 and several of those killed in action are remembered on the war memorial situated in the castle grounds.

STONEWAY STEPS
BRIDGNORTH

Bridgnorth Castle keep leans at an angle of 17°, three times more than the leaning tower of Pisa.

In 1739, St Mary's church in Shrewsbury was the setting for a stunt that went wrong when Robert Cadman, also known as Robert Kidman (1711–39), stuntman, rope slider and steeplejack, was killed performing a feat of daring.

Just before the English Civil War, in 1641, Colonel Richard Lee of Langley Hall near Acton Burnell emigrated to America. His son, General Henry Lee, served under

George Washington during the American War of Independence. Richard's grandson was the famous Confederate General Robert E. Lee.

In 2005, unverified German papers (historical Nazi documents) dating from 1941 were found, outlining details of Operation Sea Lion, Adolf Hitler's military plans for the invasion of Britain. Two quiet Shropshire towns are mentioned in the documentation as being invasion targets: Ludlow and Bridgnorth. Some experts believe that it was Hitler's intention to site his personal HQ at Apley Hall, near Bridgnorth, due to its central position in the country, and its rural location, rail connections and airfield.

The village of Condover was once home to Queen Elizabeth I's jester, Richard Tarlton, the man said to have inspired Shakespeare's Yorrick, 'A fellow of infinite jest, of most excellent fancy' whose skull features in *Hamlet*'s graveyard scene.

The Hampton Loade passenger ferry across the River Severn has been used for over 400 years. The most modern version was built in 2004 and is the UK's only reaction cable ferry.

# 9

# SPORTING
# SHROPSHIRE

**Johnny Hancocks, 1919–94:** One of Wolverhampton Wanderers's (Wolves) greatest ever footballers, number 7. Johnny was born in Oakengates on 30 April 1919 and was a winger equally happy playing outside-right or outside-left, although it was as an outside-right that he was best known. A member of Wolves's first ever Championship-winning side, Johnny was the only ever-present player in that 1953/54 season. In 1956/57, Harry Hooper had taken over Johnny's right-wing berth in the first eleven, but the little man wasn't through yet; he turned out for Wolves's reserve team, still the darling of the fans, scoring 24 goals in the Central League that season. At 5ft 4in, Johnny Hancocks was one of the smallest players around, but he packed an explosive shot into his size-4 boots. Johnny's record was incredible for a winger. In all competitions, he scored 168 goals in 378 senior games for Wolves. He joined Walsall Town from Oakengates Town just before the start of the Second World War, serving as an Army P.T. instructor during the hostilities.

He signed for Wolves on 11 May 1946 for a fee of £4,000, making his debut against Arsenal in a 6–1 win at Molineux on 31 August 1946, scoring 10 league goals and 1 in the FA Cup in his first season. This great player won 3 full England caps, scoring twice on his international debut, and also played for the Football League. He played his last first-team game for Wolves on 3 April 1956, against Aston Villa at Villa Park in a 0–0 draw, but briefly returned to the fray on Tuesday night, 11 December 1956, for the last eight minutes of the 1–1 drawn floodlit friendly against M.T.K. of Budapest, otherwise known as the 'Red Banner'. He finally hung up his boots at the ripe old footballing age of 38, when he moved to Wellington Town, now AFC Telford United, as player manager in the 1957 close season.

Johnny Hancocks was top-scorer for Wolves on three separate occasions: jointly with Jesse Pye in 1947/48 with 16 goals, in 1954/55 with 27 and in 1955/56 with 18. His 25 league goals from 42 appearances in the 1953/54 Championship season put him in joint second place with centre-forward Roy Swinbourne in Wolves's goal scoring charts. Johnny subsequently managed Southern League club Cambridge United before returning to his hometown to work for local company GKN Sankey. Johnny Hancocks died 19 February 1994, two months short of his seventy-fifth birthday.

**Joe Hart:** The 6ft 5in goalkeeper Charles Joseph John Hart was born in Shrewsbury on 19 April 1987, and attended Meole Brace School Science College. He started his professional career at Shrewsbury Town, then in the English League Division Two, helping his team to finish in tenth place, appearing in all of Town's 46 matches in the 2005/06 season. In his first season (2002/03) when still only 15 years old, Joe was a non-playing substitute, but unfortunately at the end of that season Shrewsbury Town were relegated to the Football Conference. The following season (2003/04), Joe made his senior debut on 20 April 2004, the day before his seventeenth birthday, and went on to make 2 appearances that promotion-winning season. Back in the football league in 2004/05, he made 6 appearances, conceding 4 goals. Then in 2005/06, Joe became Shrewsbury's first-choice keeper, making 46 appearances, every league game, conceding 55 goals. His first Under-19 England cap came in October 2005, when Joe was substitute for the game versus Poland.

In May 2006, Joe signed for Manchester City, and was loaned out for spells with Tranmere Rovers and Blackpool. He made his debut for the England Under-21 team on 6 February 2007, in a 2–2 draw versus Spain, coming on as substitute towards the end of the game. He lost his place as first-choice keeper for City when the club signed Shay Given, and was loaned out to Birmingham City for the entire 2009/10 season, earning a reputation as one of England's best goalkeepers. He went on to win 21 Under-21 caps. In June, England coach Fabio Capello brought Joe on as substitute for David James in a game against Trinidad & Tobago, for his first senior cap. Joe is now firmly established as England's number one.

With Manchester City he won the FA Cup in 2011 and the Premier League Title in 2011/12, and again in 2013/14.

Joe was England's 2010 World Cup third-choice keeper, but made no appearance. He played for England in the Euro 2012 and the 2014 World Cup in Brazil, and at the time of writing is England's first-choice goalkeeper with 48 full England caps.

**Sandy Lyle:** World-renowned golfer Alexander Walter Barr Lyle, MBE, was born in Shrewsbury on 9 February 1958. Sandy's father, Scotsman Alex Lyle, was professional at Hawkstone Park Golf Club, and the young man chose to represent his father's country of birth: Scotland. Sandy began playing golf when he was 3 years old, going on to represent Shropshire and Scotland at junior and amateur levels, making his debut in the British Open at the age of 16. As an amateur, he also won the Brabazon Trophy in 1975 and 1977, playing both those years in the Walker Cup, before turning professional in 1977.

The 1978 Nigerian Open was Sandy's first professional title. He has represented Europe in the Ryder Cup both as a player (five times) and as assistant captain to Ian Woosnam. He has also won the World Match Play Championship and the European Order of Merit in 1979, 1980 and 1985, finishing in the top ten nine times between 1979 and 1992. In 1987, he won the prestigious USA Tournament Player's Championship. Sandy Lyle won the 2011 ISPS Honda Senior World Championship, in China, and now plays on the Senior's Tour in Europe. In a distinguished career, Sandy Lyle has won two major championships – the Masters and the British Open. He now lives in Scotland with his wife and children.

**Sir Gordon Richards, 1904–86:** Champion jockey Gordon Richards was born on 5 May 1904 and raised in Donnington Wood. He was the first English flat-race jockey to ride 4,000 winners, and topped the winning jockey list for 26 out of 34 seasons between 1921 and 1954. In all, he won 4,870 races, then a world record, and was the first jockey to be knighted. His one and only Derby win came in 1954. He won the St Leger 5 times, and the 2,000 Guineas 3 times. Injury finally forced him to retire as a jockey, becoming a trainer and later a racing manager. Sir Gordon Richards died on 10 November 1986, in Kintbury, Berkshire.

**Captain Matthew Webb, 1848–83:** Matthew Webb, steamship captain and famous swimmer, was born in Dawley, Shropshire, on 19 January 1848, the eldest of twelve children.

On 24 August 1875, Webb became the first person to swim the 26 miles from Dover to Calais without the use of artificial aids – modern estimates suggest that he probably swam close to 39 miles when taking into account tidal currents. The swim took him twenty-one hours and forty-five minutes. The story goes that in 1873, whilst serving in the merchant navy, Captain Webb of the steamship *Emerald* was inspired to try to swim the English Channel when he read of J.B. Johnson's failed attempt. His first attempt failed but, dressed in a Victorian one-piece bathing costume and his body covered in porpoise oil, Webb set off on his second attempt by diving into the sea from the Admiralty Pier at Dover. Captain Webb's historic achievement made him a hero in Great Britain and the world over. He gave up his career in the merchant navy in favour of professional endurance swimming.

His sad death came on 24 July 1883 during an attempt to swim across the Niagara River directly beneath Niagara Falls. Shortly after entering the water, Webb was caught in the vicious current and was dragged under. His mangled body was found four days later some distance downstream. He was buried at Oakwood Cemetery, Niagara Falls.

In Dawley there are well-known pictures of a pig sat on a wall. This pig apparently placed his front trotters on top of the wall of its sty and sat to watch the brass band as it passed by, leading the procession when Captain Matthew Webb returned in triumph after his successful swim of the English Channel. Gornal in the Black Country also claim this piggy feat.

**Ian Woosnam:** Golfer Ian Harold Woosnam, OBE, was born in Oswestry on 2 March 1958. Woosie represented Europe in the Ryder Cup, and amongst many other titles he went on to win one of the five Majors, the US Masters in 1991. He started playing golf at Llanymynech Golf Club, representing Shropshire County Boys in an eight-man team that included Sandy Lyle and Duncan Hamling of Bridgnorth. The other boys were Kevin Beamond, Mike Simcock, Alan Strange, Phillip Gee and James Williams.

Turning professional in 1976, Woosnam joined the European tour in 1979, topping the European Order of Merit in 1987 and again in 1990, when his global earnings topped £1 million. From 7 April 1991 until 21 March 1992, for fifty weeks, Woosie was ranked the number one golfer in the world. After suffering a loss of form later that decade, in 2001 Woosie looked like he might win the British Open, until a freak incident robbed him of his chance. Having finished the third round as joint leader, on 6 under par, along with three others, Woosnam was hit with a 2-shot penalty. His caddie, Myles Byrne, had failed to ensure that no more than the maximum fourteen clubs were in his boss's golf bag for the final round – there were fifteen. The penalty robbed Ian of the momentum that had carried him so well through the earlier rounds, and he eventually finished four shots behind David Duval. Woosnam played in eight consecutive Ryder Cups between 1983 and 1997. In 2002, he was vice-captain of the European team, and was captain in 2006. He is the only golfer to win the Order of Merit at both regular and senior level.

**Billy Wright, 1924–94:** William Ambrose Wright, CBE, captain, left-half, centre-half, right-back and left-back, is one of England's greatest ever footballers. Born in Ironbridge on 6 February 1924, Billy Wright, CBE, was a marvellous man, a true ambassador of the sport and a truly great footballer. For Wolverhampton Wanderers he made a total of 541 appearances, scoring 16 goals. He joined the ground staff in 1938, after initially being turned down by manager Major Buckley for being too small. He made his debut for Wolves against West Bromwich Albion in a 5–3 defeat at The Hawthorns on 23 September 1939, before turning professional in 1941.

Billy Wright went on to win 105 full England caps, his first in 1946, captaining England on 90 occasions, and playing in the final of three World Cups. He also won an England 'B' cap and was selected for the Football League on 21 occasions. And, of course, he won an FA Cup and 3 First Division Championships with Wolves. In his exemplary twenty-year first-class career, Billy was never booked or sent off. He was a great man, a great Wolves and England captain. It was at the start of the 1959/60 season that this Wolves legend, then aged 35, dropped a bombshell by announcing his retirement. He reputedly told a reporter, 'Yes, this is it. I have had a wonderful run with a wonderful club and I want to finish while I am still at the top.' Manager Stan Cullis was reported to have said that under no circumstances would he ask Billy to play for the reserves in the Central League team; he wanted him to finish as a first-team player. Billy played his farewell match at Molineux in Wolves's colours in the pre-season charity practice match on Saturday, 8 August 1959. Although Billy's news was bad for Wolves, it was good for charity as a larger than normal number of fans was expected to turn out in honour of their captain: 20,000, twice the usual, came to Molineux to witness Billy's swan song. The game was an emotional affair, with the players forming a guard of honour. As a mark of respect, Billy was switched from the whites – the second eleven – to the colours – the first-team – for his last Molineux match. The whites won 4–2. In a later interview Billy acknowledged that he had told reporters the previous April that he reckoned he was good for another season at least, but added that since he had got his England hundred, and had been awarded the CBE, he had thought it over and decided it was the time to quit. Stan Cullis wanted Billy to take over as his chief coach, with specific responsibility for coaching the club's youngsters. Billy hadn't yet decided, but had confirmed that he would not move to another club, saying, 'How can I play for anyone else after Wolves?'

What more can be said about Billy Wright that hasn't already been said? A true gentleman, he always had time to sign autographs, always had time for the fans. Voted 'Footballer of the Year' in 1951/52 and runner-up 'European Footballer of the Year' in 1956/57, Billy won everything and achieved everything in his long and illustrious career. He was the David Beckham of his day, Captain of England and married to one of the best-known faces in show business, Joy Beverley of the Beverley Sisters singing trio. Elected a life member of the FA, Billy was the rock that Stan Cullis built his team around.

In October 1960, Billy was appointed manager of the England Youth team, and after this manager of England Under-23s. He went on to manage Arsenal in May 1962, before becoming Head of Sport at ATV, and then at Central TV, and subsequently a director of his beloved Wolverhampton Wanderers. Billy Wright died aged 70 on 3 September 1994, a great loss to England and sport in general.

"FATTY"
FOULKE
SHEFFIELD UNITED
GOALKEEPER

**William 'Fatty' Foulke, 1874–1916:** Born in Dawley on 12 April 1874, William Henry Foulke was a giant in the world of goalkeepers. At 6ft 2in, he played football for Blackwell Colliery, transferring to Sheffield United for a fee of £20. He went on to win 2 FA Cup Winners medals with The Blades, with whom he also won the League in the 1897/98 season. Bill won 1 cap against Wales on 29 March 1897, a game England won 4–0. His trick was to pull down the crossbar, bending down the bar to prevent a goal being scored by the opposition; in one game he pulled so hard he broke the crossbar in half. In 1895, Foulke weighed only 12 stones 10lb, but as he grew older so did his girth, until his weight topped 25 stone, and thus he was nicknamed 'Fatty Foulke' and 'Colossus'. In May 1905 he was transferred to Chelsea for £50, moving on the Bradford City for a fee of £50 after 35 games for the Blues. He also played cricket for Blackwell Colliery in the Derbyshire League, and turned out for Derbyshire County Cricket Club, but gave it up after hurting his hand. He was once described as 'A leviathan at 22 stone with the agility of a bantam'. Bill Foulke died on 1 May 1916.

**David Preece, 1963–2007:** Midfielder David William Preece was born in Bridgnorth on 28 May 1963. He began his footballing career at Walsall FC, turning professional in 1980, and making his first team debut in 1981. Three years later he was transferred to Luton Town, where he had an illustrious career, winning the League Cup in 1988, and 3 England B caps. In 1995 he moved to Derby County on a free transfer, where he was loaned out to Birmingham City and Swindon Town, before joining Cambridge United in 1996, again on a free transfer, subsequently being appointed Assistant Manager to Roy McFarland. In August 2001 he joined Torquay United as player/ coach, then on to Enfield and Stevenage Borough. In May 2003, he was appointed first-team coach of Telford United, a year later he joined Walton & Hersham as assistant manager. Sadly, David Preece died on 20 July 2007 after a short illness. The family stand at Luton Town's Kenilworth Road Football Ground has since been named 'The David Preece Stand' in his memory.

**Richie Woodall:** World champion boxer Richie Woodhall was born in Birmingham on 17 April 1968. His family moved to Telford when Richie was 2. He won a gold medal at the 1990 Commonwealth Games in Auckland, and a bronze at the 1988 Olympics in Seoul, both as a light-middleweight. Richie Woodhall turned professional in 1990 and won the vacant Commonwealth Middleweight Championship in 1992, holding the title until 1995. That year he defeated Italy's Silvio Branco for the European Boxing Union Middleweight Championship, which he held until 1996, when Richie fought champion Keith Holmes for the World Boxing Council Middleweight title. Here he was stopped on a technical knock-out in the twelfth round, having gone into this fight carrying an injury. In 1998, after moving up a weight, he fought for and won the WBC Super-Middleweight Championship, successfully defending the title twice, before losing to Markus Beyer in 1999. On 16 December 2000, he fought an epic bout against his friend Welshman Joe Calzaghe, before retiring from boxing. In more recent times Richie Woodhall has worked on radio and TV with the BBC, Sky Sports and Setanta Sports, finding time to be involved with the 2012 London Olympics, coaching the Olympic boxing squad. Richie also appeared as Brad Pitt's body double in the movie *Snatch*.

**Gerry Harris:** Gerald William Harris was born in Claverley on 8 October 1935. He signed amateur forms for Wolverhampton

Wanderers after an unsuccessful trial for West Bromwich Albion in 1953. In January 1954, Gerry turned professional, making his first-team debut against Luton Town on 29 August 1956, a game Wolves won 5–4. Gerry hardly missed a game between 1956 and 1961, during which time Wolves won 2 successive League Championships – in 1957/58 and 1958/59 – only failing to make it 3 in a row by one point in 1959/60, though they did win the FA Cup that season. Gerry Harris also had the distinction of playing for Wolves in every game in the European Cup. In all, he made 270 appearances for Wolves. In 1966, Gerry moved a few miles down the road to Walsall FC, but sadly injury brought his career to an end a year later.

**Joe Berks, 1777–1812:** A bare-knuckle boxer of great strength, Joe was born in Wem in 1777, and was immortalised by Sir Arthur Conan Doyle as a character in his story 'The House of Timperley'. He served under Lord Rowland Hill in the Peninsular War, in which he was killed in 1812.

**Alison Williamson:** International and Shropshire County Archer Alison Williamson holds the distinction of competing at 6 consecutive Olympic Games: Barcelona 1992, finishing seventh; Atlanta 1996; Sydney 2000; Athens 2004, where she won a bronze medal; Beijing 2008; and London 2012 as a wild card selection.

## FOOTBALL

At the time of writing, the county has no football teams in the upper echelons of the football league.

Shrewsbury Town FC, founded in 1886, home ground Greenhous Meadow (a UEFA category 4 stadium), is the county's highest-placed club, playing in League One (level 3). Oh oh! Just as I write this, the Shrews have been relegated to League Two (level 4). Let's hope they can get back next season.

AFC Telford United have just been promoted from the Skrill Conference North (level 6) to the Skrill Conference Premier (level 5). Their home ground is the New Buck's Head. Founded as Wellington Town in 1892, the club changed its name in 1962 to Telford United FC. The club folded in 2004, re-emerging as AFC Telford United and, as I say, hip hip hooray for Telford's promotion!

Playing at level 8 are Market Drayton Town, Northern Premier League Division One South.

We had four, now we have five, of Shropshire football clubs playing in the West Midlands (Regional) League Premier Division (level 10): Ellesmere Rangers, Shawbury United, Shifnal Town, Wellington Amateurs, and AFC Bridgnorth have just been promoted from level 11.

One level down in the West Midlands (Regional) League Division One (level 11), we have Hanwood United, Haughmond, St Martins and Wem Town.

In the West Midlands (Regional) League Division Two (level 12) we have AFRC Ludlow and Newport Town.

Oswestry Town FC, founded in 1876, have the distinction of being the only English football club to play in Wales. The club was originally founded in 1860, making it one of the oldest in the world. Their first game, on 25 March 1876, was played at Hamilton Crescent, Partick, Glasgow; they lost 4–0 to Scotland. The game was organised by a Welsh solicitor, Samuel Llewelyn Kenrick (1847–29 May 1933).

What happened to the football club after the start of the millennium is quite an involved story, but it boils down to the fact that in 2003 financially challenged Oswestry Town amalgamated with Total Network Solutions FC (TNS) to form The New Saints of Oswestry Town and Llansantffraid Football club (in Welsh: Clwb Pel-droed y seintiall Newydd). Known as The New Saints, they played again in the Welsh Premier League at Park Hall Oswestry, winning the league in 2013/14, and thus qualifying for the Champion's League. Llansantffraid is a mere 8 miles from Oswestry.

The 1966 World Cup winners England trained at Lilleshall Sports Centre.

## CRICKET

Shropshire play in the Minor County Cricket League, winning the Minor Counties Championship in 1973, and the MCCA Knockout Trophy in 2010. According to Rowland Bowen, the first recorded cricket match to be played in Shropshire was in 1794.

## RUGBY FOOTBALL

The North Midlands Rugby Football Union includes the following affiliated RFC clubs: Bridgnorth, Bishop's Castle and Onny Valley, Clee Hill, Church Stretton, Cleobury Mortimer, Highley, Ludlow, Market Drayton, Newport (Salop), Oswestry, Shrewsbury, Telford Hornets and Whitchurch.

## HORSE RACING

At Bromfield, Ludlow.

## MOTOR RACING

At the motocross circuit at Loton Park Hill Climb, Hawkstone Park.

## AMERICAN FOOTBALL

We have one team in Shropshire: Shropshire Revolution, founded in 2006, based in Telford. They play in the British American Football League.

## ICE HOCKEY

Telford Tigers, play – guess where? At the Telford Ice Rink, which was opened by HRH Princess Anne in October 1984, in time for the 1985/86 season. Telford Tigers Ice Hockey Club Ltd was formed by Central ITV Head of Sport Gary Newbon and comedian Dave Ismay, the latter as chairman. The player coach was that great percussionist, Canadian defenceman Chuck Taylor. Newbon and Taylor were previously involved with the Barons. The Tigers finished third in the First Division of the British Hockey League in that inaugural season and Chuck Taylor made the All Star Team. For the 1987/88 season, the First Division split into two sections – North and South Conferences. Telford Tigers won the Southern Conference by 2 points, then in the play-off went on to beat Northern Conference Champions Cleveland Bombers 21–14 on aggregate to take the overall title. Chuck Taylor was named Coach of the Year.

The following season was not good for Telford. The team struggled both on and off the ice eventually, being put into liquidation that summer. The club reformed in 1990 with Chuck Taylor as managing director, but in 1994 Chuck left for Nottingham. The club continued, and in the summer of 1999 re-emerged as Telford Timberwolves, reforming in 2001 as Telford Wild Foxes. It kept this name until 2005, when it reverted to Telford Tigers, who play in the English Premier League.

## OLYMPIC GAMES

Much Wenlock will forever be linked with the modern Olympic Games due to Doctor William Penny Brookes. In 1850 the good doctor, a pioneer of temperance and appalled by the abundance of heavy drinking and fighting, launched the first annual games in the town (see People, Dr William Penny Brookes).

## ANGLING

With so much water in the county, there are hundreds of suitable stretches for keen piscatorialists. The Shropshire Angler's Federation, formed in 1921, has all the details on their website.

## CROWN GREEN BOWLING

Again, there are numerous clubs in the county. The website of the Shropshire Crown Green Bowling Association has lots of information.

# GOLF

The county has many 18-hole golf courses. The oldest in the county
is Church Stretton Golf Club, which opened in 1898. Others include
Bridgnorth, Shifnal, Worfield, Hawkstone Park, Lilleshall Hall,
Llanymynech, Ludlow, Market Drayton, Meole Brace (municipal),
Oswestry, Shrewsbury, Great Hay at Telford, Wrekin, Aqualate,
Arscott, Astbury Hall, The Brow, Chesterton Valley, Mile End,
The Shropshire and Worfield.

## HOT AIR BALLOONING

At 4.10 a.m. local time on 2 July 1987, Virgin Atlantic Flyer piloted by Per Lindstrand and Richard Branson lifted off from Sugar Loaf Mountain in western Maine, USA, to begin an attempt to fly a hot-air balloon across the Atlantic, over 3,000 miles. The entire balloon had been fabricated at Thunder & Colt's factory in Oswestry. Thirty-one hours later the balloon began its descent over Northern Ireland, touching down near Limavady. The balloon was dragged along the ground for over 50yds, then climbed back to 6,000ft. In the end, they landed safely.

# 10

# SHROPSHIRE MURDERS

Jack Blondell, nicknamed Blaudy Jack or Bloudie Jacke of Shrewsberrie, was a twelfth-century serial murderer who lived on the site of Shrewsbury Castle before it was rebuilt. Jack married a lot of women – possibly eight – who, when he got tired of them, mysteriously disappeared. The sister of his eighth wife grew suspicious and spoke of her concerns to a watchman. A search led to a sickening discovery: a cabinet full of rotting human remains. Jack had kept the fingers and toes of his victims tied in bunches of five as gruesome mementoes. He was arrested, tried and found guilty, then hung, drawn and quartered on Wyle Cop. His ghost is said to haunt the castle grounds.

In 1841, a 25-year-old man from Birmingham, Joseph Misters, was found guilty of attempted murder and sentenced to be hanged. The crime had taken place seven months earlier in Ludlow, where the young chap had tried to slice open the throat of a man coincidentally named John Ludlow, a cattle salesman. Ludlow's business meant he had a large sum of money on his person. The lad from Birmingham had spotted Ludlow, and had followed him for some time, planning to rob the cattle dealer at the Angel Inn, where John Ludlow, a creature of habit, had a regular room when in town. On the night of 19 August 1840, Joseph Misters hid in Ludlow's room, remaining undetected until its occupant was sound asleep. Unfortunately for Joseph Misters, John Ludlow was not in his usual room that fateful night. Sleeping in the bed was a travelling businessman named William Mackreth.

In the early hours Joseph Misters crept from his hiding place and tried to slit the sleeper's throat, but his attempt failed when Mackreth leaped out of bed having felt the sting of Misters's razor on his skin.

His quick reaction saved his life, and his attacker fled empty handed. Shocked and unable to speak, his throat and face severely cut, Mackreth was at first thought to have attempted to commit suicide. He was able to write down what had happened, and Joseph Misters was arrested that same night. Stoutly proclaiming his innocence throughout his trial, Misters appeared to be convinced that he would be found not guilty of the crime, and spoke of his intention to travel to Peru upon his release. But the evidence against him was strong. The dust underneath Mackreth's bed showed that someone had been hiding there, and a trail of bloodstains led from Mackreth's room to Misters's own room, where bloodstained clothing was found. Finally, the suspected murder weapon, a black-handled cut-throat razor, matched a set found at Misters's home in Birmingham, which was missing one razor. On 3 April 1837, Joseph Misters was executed in front of the county prison at Shrewsbury.

And now for a tale of betrayal. Some time in 1827, petty criminal James Harrison was beaten and strangled by John Cox (aged 26) and James Pugh (aged 19) while Cox's younger brother, Robert, kept a lookout. Harrison's lifeless body was buried in a ditch.

Harrison was to have been the main witness to the trial of Thomas Ellison for theft, punishable by death, but when the witness failed to appear Ellison was discharged. The killers had been paid to murder Harrison by Ellison's mother, Ann Harris, to save her son from the hangman. Almost a year later, Ellison was arrested for stealing fowl, and in an attempt to obtain a pardon for this crime he grassed up the Cox brothers, who incidentally were his brothers-in-law, plus their father, John Cox Senior, James Pugh and his own mother. In court he gave evidence that saw all five found guilty. John Cox Jr and Pugh were hanged in front of Shrewsbury jail on 4 August 1828. Robert Cox's death sentence was commuted to transportation to Tasmania. Ditto John Cox Snr, who was transported to Australia. Ann Harris was executed on 16 August 1828 – the last woman to be publicly executed in Shrewsbury. Sir Arthur Conan Doyle wrote a piece about this sad tale entitled 'The Bravoes of Market Drayton'.

Hanged alongside Cox and Pugh was a vicious thug by the name of William Steventon, a collier known locally as 'Billy Sugar', and his is a frightful story.

These days Oldbury and Halesowen are situated in the West Midlands, but in 1828 Oldbury was part of the parish of Halesowen, both being in a detached part of Shropshire. The Old Whimsey Inn in Oldbury was a favourite haunt of 'Billy Sugar' and many other unsavoury characters, including hard-working, hard-drinking coal miners – a rough, tough fraternity. William Steventon had somehow managed to avoid arrest despite having six or seven warrants issued against him over the previous two years – he swore that he would butcher any lawman who tried to arrest him.

On the evening of 31 March 1828, the sergeant of Oldbury Court and local jailer, John Horton of Halesowen, entered the pub and made an attempt to arrest Steventon. At first Steventon was compliant, asking the officer to be allowed home to clean himself up. Horton agreed, but when Steventon returned he slapped one hand over the lawman's mouth and plunged a long-bladed knife into Horton's liver. He died in agony the next day.

A murder warrant was issued with a reward of 30 guineas. In the meantime Steventon escaped, making his way across Shropshire and on into Wales. But on 23 April 1828, he was arrested in Pontypool, subdued by four officers and taken to Oldbury, and thence to Shrewsbury Gaol. He was of course found guilty and executed on 4 August along with Cox and Pugh, in front of an estimated crowd of 5,000 spectators.

# 11

# GHOSTS, MYTHS AND LEGENDS

## GHOSTS

Shropshire has numerous ghosts, here are just a few:

The Roman Soldier of Bomere, near Condover, can lay claim to being Shropshire's oldest ghost. This phantom apparently wanders around looking for his sweetheart, who was drowned in a sudden flood. The soldier appears whenever Easter Day falls on the same day as it did the year he died.

The legend of the Black Pool and the White Lady of Longnor is an all-too-frequent tale of woe. This White Lady is said to be the ghost of a jilted pregnant young bride, wearing her wedding dress, who, heartbroken and overcome with grief and shame, committed suicide by drowning herself in the Black Pool. She appears on a bridge crossing a tributary of the Cound Brook and stands for a moment or two before seeming to float away over the bridge and into the water. The Black Pool is no longer there, it was filled in years ago. In times past the phantom would appear when there was a party nearby, and on one occasion, a reveller said he had seen her and tried to dance with her, stunned when his arms passed right through her body. (He may have been drunk!)

There is another White Lady, this one of Kilsall, whose spirit haunts the dark walk beside a pool in the grounds of Kilsall Hall. She is said to have drowned herself for the same reason as the White Lady of Longnor.

At dusk in the Onny Valley there is a ghostly procession known as the Ratlinghope Funeral Cortège. Two black-plumed horses pull a magnificent carriage driven by pallbearers wearing top hats, which glides slowly along the narrow lane, across the bridge and past the public house to wend its way up the hill out of the village, eventually disappearing from view. No one knows who lies in the coffin or where the cortège is heading, nor is there any record of such a funeral.

A tragic tale occurred one night in the little hamlet of Astley Abbots on the Broseley Road just outside Bridgnorth. A man was driving home when in the distance he saw a woman crossing the road. She was around 5ft tall, wearing dark drab clothes, a shawl wrapped tight around her head, and her long skirt touched the ground. When the driver drew nearer, the woman simply vanished. He was told later he had seen the ghost of Hannah Phillips, a young woman who had lived on the other side of the River Severn, and was due to be married at Astley Abbots church. A day or two before her wedding, while crossing the ford to return home after going to the church to help get everything ready, she slipped and fell into the river, never to be seen alive again. Her ghost still makes that fateful journey.

On a wall of the Bassa Villa restaurant in Bridgnorth, which backs on to the River Severn at the bottom of the Cartway, there is a plaque that tells the tragic story of a children's game gone wrong. In the 1600s during a game of hide and seek, a boy and a girl, brother and sister, found themselves accidentally locked in the cellar of the house. When the river flooded and burst its banks the children had no means of escape and were drowned. Grief stricken, the children's mother and father commissioned marble images of the children to be erected. The ghost of the tormented mother, known as the Black Lady, wanders the house, still grieving for her lost children. On occasions she has been heard crying softly, and at other times she has been heard laughing, perhaps remembering happier times.

The old carpet factory in Bridgnorth, located on the site of an old priory, had its share of ghostly apparitions before it was demolished. Late one night a lady, the last person in the building, was startled

by a shadowy figure in the old part of the factory. It was 'Old Mo'. The phantom was wearing a white monk's habit. She watched in terror as the apparition made its way up the steps from the basement towards her, but when the figure reached the top it turned on its heels and went back down again.

During the reign of King Henry II, one of the ladies of the household of Ludlow Castle, Marion de la Bruyere, took a lover to her bed. When the castle was besieged by the de Lacys, Marion's lover turned out to be one of the enemy. During the siege, lovelorn Marion lowered a rope for her secret lover, which he climbed, bringing soldiers with him. When she realised that her lover had betrayed her, Marion stabbed him with his own sword, then hurled herself from the window of the tower, to die on the rocks below. Her shadowy ghost has been seen on the stairway of the Hanging Tower as she re-enacts her tragic dive. She is known as the Grey Lady of Ludlow Castle and her lover's death cries have also been heard – it's another tragic tale of a lover's betrayal.

In the latter part of the reign of Queen Victoria, a gentleman employer was walking along Benthall Edge when he was set upon by a gang of ruffians, who robbed him of the money he was carrying – the wages for his workers at his limestone works on the Edge. He was bound, gagged and then thrown into a pit, which the thieves then covered with a heavy stone. When the employer failed to arrive at his works a search party was sent to find him. Sadly, in his attempt to escape, the stone had slipped and crushed him to death. People walking along the edge still hear the man's vain calls for help.

Shrewsbury's wonderful Dingle is haunted by the ghost of a woman named Mrs Foxall, who in 1647 was burned at the stake for murdering her husband.

On a freezing morning late in the 1880s, part of the glass roof of Shrewsbury's Railway Station collapsed, crushing the carriage of a Thomas Thomas, coal merchant, MP, and town councillor, with him inside, killing him and injuring his horse. Near the ramp at the Castle Street platform three entrance, the shadowy phantom has been seen, either sitting or standing, still waiting for the London train.

The main hall of sixteenth-century Wilderhope Manor is said to be haunted by the ghost of a tall cavalier, wearing a wide-brimmed cavalier hat complete with plume, cloak and thigh-length boots, who stands in a doorway for a time before walking across the hall to disappear through a wall.

Also at Wilderhope is the ghost of a young lady who appears occasionally. Apparently she smiles, then screams like a banshee.

From tiny windows in the magnificent twin gatehouse towers of Whittington Castle, the ghostly faces of two small children have regularly been seen.

On spooky, misty nights in the churchyard and on the land where once stood the old castle at Ruyton, you might see the headless horseman riding towards the castle keep, mist swirling around man and horse, who then disappear into it.

In a hangar at RAF Cosford there is an Avro Lincoln long-range heavy bomber, where the ghost of a young man has been regularly seen. In 1991, the BBC sent a crew to investigate the phenomenon – they recorded lots of spooky sounds but no visual images.

In the Prince Rupert Hotel in Shrewsbury there have been night-time sightings of a phantom wearing a long white nightshirt and carrying a candle.

One of the oddest ghostly claims is that of a monk who appears to float across the street in Shrewsbury from St Chad's church to the buildings on the opposite side of the road. The explanation is that there was once a walkway from the church to the lodgings across the road.

Anyone arriving at Tyrley Middle Lock in the middle of the night might meet the friendly resident ghost, who will close the lock gates behind you.

Bridge 39, near Norbury Junction, Grub Street cutting, on the 67-mile long Shropshire Union Canal, is said to be haunted by the ghost of a boatman who drowned in the nineteenth century. He is known as the 'Monkey Man' after his black shaggy-coated appearance.

There are ghost walks available in many Shropshire towns if you feel brave enough!

## MYTHS, LEGENDS AND ODDITIES

On hot summer nights on top of the Stiperstones, the smell of brimstone in the air warns the wary traveller that Beelzebub himself sits upon his lofty throne – the ragged peak called the Devil's Chair – surveying his kingdom. One tale suggests that the rocky outcrop was formed when old Beelzebub was taking a quick break from his work filling in the valley at Hell's Gutter. Getting up, his apron strings broke and, cursing, he dropped the rocks where they now stand. Another legend has is that the Devil's work is not yet complete. Disliking Shropshire more than any other county, he brings rocks to dump on the hills in the hope that Shropshire will one day sink into the sea.

Not far from Easthope on Wenlock Edge there is a steep cliff with a cave, between Presthope and Lutwyche Hall, where lives the ghost of Old Ippikin, a thirteenth-century robber knight. He was a fierce man of sour temper and evil looks, and anyone daft enough to summon him by shouting, 'Ippikin, Ippikin, keep away with your long chin,' will come to some harm. The consequences might prove to be fatal. Some say that Ippikin was a sorceror who renewed his life every seventy years and he, with his gang of bandits, terrorised the locality, and hoarded a pile of treasure, coins and jewels in the cave. The legend sprang from a huge storm, when lightning struck a huge rock overhanging the cave, causing it to topple and fall, crashing down to block the cave entrance and allegedly trapping Ippikin and his murderous gang inside – a well-deserved comeuppance.

Edgar Allan Poe might have penned this one. During a Christmas Eve party, in an old timber-framed house on the outskirts of the village of Minsterley, the talk at the dinner table was halted by a terrifying sound outside. The silence in the room was filled by a piercing scream and blind panic set in. The guests fought each other as they scrambled to reach the door and in the confusion the host disappeared. Later, one brave man returned to the room. Inside he was faced by a sight that chilled his bones. He discovered the host lying dead under an upturned table: his face and his clothes, plus the surrounding furniture had been shredded by what looked to be the rake of a giant claw, which was found embedded in his eye – the Devil's Talon!

Convicted of the murder of his employer, Lord Knyvett, the condemned butler of Condover Hall swore his innocence to the end. He cursed the descendants of Knyvett's family as he stood on the scaffold awaiting the hangman's pleasure, vowing that they would not prosper as long as they lived in the hall. He had been condemned by the lying son of Lord Knyvett, who in reality had stabbed his own father to death then accused the butler. The mortally wounded Lord Kynvett had stumbled down the basement stairs, leaving a bloody handprint on the stone wall, a red stain that proved impossible to wash away, for each time it was removed it reappeared. Finally, it had to be chipped off the stone. In more recent times, footsteps and the sound of doors closing have been heard at night, and a man and a woman dressed in Victorian clothing have been seen.

On the Stiperstones you may hear or even see Wild Edric, the rebel Saxon thane imprisoned underground as punishment for siding with William the Conqueror. Mounted on galloping horses, he and his men ride to war, unable to rest until all the wrongs in the country are put right (see People).

There are quite a few legends about the infamous Wild Edric. A popular one is that he got lost on his way home from hunting alone in Clun Forest. Hearing music and singing he came across an ancient dwelling. He peered through a window and saw six tall, fair maidens dancing around the most beautiful girl imaginable. Edric instantly fell in love, and rushed inside, but as he grabbed the girl the six others turned into screaming harpies, who attacked him with sharp talons. He escaped with the girl, whose name was Godda, and took her to his hall, soon realising that she was from the faerie world.

For three days and nights she said not a word, refusing food and drink. On the fourth day she spoke, calling him her love, and promised she would marry him and he would live a long and happy life, providing he never criticised her six sisters or the place he found her. The pair were married and when King William I heard the story he invited the couple to court. Back home, they lived happily until Edric returned from hunting one day to find she was not at home. When she returned, he forgot his promise and accused her six sisters of enticing her away. She gazed at him sadly then disappeared. Grief stricken, he searched and searched, but no trace of her was found. Edric wept and lamented her loss, and finally pined away and died.

Some say that Edric lives on in the half-world between fantasy and reality, that he was banished to wander the underworld for eternity because he swore allegiance to the Normans. Lead miners claimed that noises in underground galleries were Edric knocking, leading them to the richest ore.

Another legend is that Edric leads the Wild Hunt across stormy skies. It is said that a few months prior to the start of the Crimean War, in the middle of the nineteenth century, a young girl from Rorrington claimed that she and her father, a miner, had heard the dreadful cry of a huntsman's horn coming from the heavens. They had looked up and witnessed a frightening sight – Wild Edric and his faerie queen Godda riding across the sky. The girl described Edric as having short dark hair from which spouted a green and white feather, his coat and cloak were also green, and a sword and hunting horn hung from his belt. Godda's long golden hair hung to her waist and around her head was a band of white linen. Her dress was also green, and a short dagger hung from her belt. The pair watched in awe until the spectral hunt had disappeared. Neither the girl nor her father suffered any ill effects, and they obviously had fantastic eyesight! Legend has it that Edric's Wild Hunt appears before a war, riding in the direction of the conflict. It's claimed that the ghostly couple were seen before the First World War, though not the second.

In the church at Middleton there is a carving that tells of the great drought that swept through Shropshire in the Middle Ages, when the starving population were helped by a kind faerie queen. One day, she led a beautiful white cow to graze on Stapeley Hill, telling the people that the magical cow would produce milk enough for everyone, but restricting the population to only one vessel-full at a time. Unfortunately, one night at midnight, Mitchell, a wicked witch who hated the faerie queen, milked the cow using a pail that had no bottom. Thunder and lightning ensued, illuminating the river of milk that gushed away down the hillside. The cow got angry at this waste of her milk and kicked the witch before galloping away, never to return to Shropshire. Apparently it fled to Warwickshire, where it became the Dun Cow. The faerie queen then caught the witch and took revenge. Next morning, there was no trace of Mitchell, but where she had stood there was now a stone pillar. The legend is that other stones were placed to pen in the witch so that she could never escape. This place is known as Mitchell's Fold.

And now for the best legend of all ...

# THE LEGEND OF KING ARTHUR AND SHROPSHIRE

Forget those medieval Arthurian romances of the twelfth to the fifteenth centuries, which some say are all myth and legend, but of course it should be remembered that most legends have some basis in fact. Meet the real King Arthur – 'Owain Ddantgwyn – Artur – The Bear', a great king of Powys in the Dark Ages.

Yes, I know that many places in England claim to be the true site of the legend of King Arthur. Tintagel in Cornwall has the most marketed one; however, the county of Shropshire has a claim that is hard to deny. Here's why:

Once upon a time in the annals of what is now called Britain, in a time now known as the Dark Ages, after the Roman legions departed these shores, there lived a tribe whose territory included much of modern Shropshire. Their king was Gogyrfan, whose seat of power was based at Old Oswestry Hill Fort (its Welsh name means the Old City; its alternative name is Caer Ogyrfan, translating as the City of Gogyrfan). King Gogyrfan was the legendary father of the Lady Ganhumara (Guinevere), who married a British warlord by the name of Owain Ddantgwen or Artur (son of Einon Yrth ap Cunedda) King of Powys, whose capital was at Virconium (Wroxeter), the fourth-largest city in Roman Britain. In AD 493, Artur led a force of Britons to a decisive victory over the invading Anglo-Saxons at Badon. Artur was not his name; it was a title, meaning 'the Bear'. Wroxeter (Viroconium) is therefore Camelot. Caer Caradoc (Avalon) is the place where Artur drew the magical sword Excalibur from the stone to claim his rightful place as king.

According to Graham Phillips and Martin Keatman in their book *King Arthur: The True Story* (1992), there are ancient manuscripts that have been unearthed in the British Library, written much earlier than the medieval romances, that suggest the historical existence of Artur, King of Powys, a kingdom that once included Shropshire and Central Wales.

Excavations at Wroxeter show the city to have been amongst the most sophisticated in the country in the fifth century, a time when Artur was Britain's most powerful king. One of the British Library manuscripts, from the tenth century, records that Wroxeter was occupied around AD 493 by Owain Ddantgwyn, a late fifth-century king of Powys and an important warlord, and if this isn't enough, there is contemporary historical evidence that Owain was actually known as Artur. A ninth-century poem names the burial site of the King of Powys as the 'Churches of Bassa' – modern-day Baschurch. Following Artur's death some time around AD 520, a great civil war broke out between the rival claimants to the kingdom, and it appears that Artur's son Cuneglasus may have abandoned Wroxeter for the more defensible site of the Wrekin.

In some early Welsh poetry there are suggestions that the crown jewels and treasures of the kingdom of Powys were hidden in Much Wenlock Priory. There is also a legend that tells of the magical Cauldron of Di-wrnach, which is said to contain all the treasures of Britain, including a magical sword, and lies hidden in Caradoc's Cave below the summit of Caer Caradoc. There is also the Welsh tale of Culhwch and Olwen, which tells of Artur's search for the Cauldron of Di-wrnach, and 'The Spoils of Annwn', which tells how Artur recovered the cauldron from the mystical isle of Annwn.

These tales from perhaps as early as AD 900 appear to have been at the heart of the Arthurian legend, with its themes of Artur, Avalon and the quest for the Holy Grail.

Moving on to the search for the Holy Grail. Whittington Castle was built by Pain (or Payne) Perevil, who was married to Lynette. a granddaughter of the Welsh Baron Cadfarch and direct descendant of Owain Ddantgwyn (Artur). Legend has it that the chapel of Whittington Castle is the hiding place of the Holy Grail. The grotto at Hawkstone Park has also been linked with the Holy Grail. In 1920, a small stone cup was found hidden in the base of a statue of an eagle there.

I leave it to the reader to make up his or her own mind.

# 12

# BATTLES, SKIRMISHES AND SIEGES

## SHROPSHIRE IN THE DARK AGES

For a long time before the Norman invasion in 1066, Shropshire had held a key position on the turbulent border between England and Wales. The Welsh Marches were the scene of multiple raids and sieges over the centuries. Pre-1066, it was the Saxons and the Welsh that were at each other's throats. Then came the Normans, who took many years to bring the indigenous peoples into line. The constant threat of a Welsh uprising prompted a period of castle building, in conjunction with the strengthening of existing inadequate fortifications.

**The Battle of Caer Caradoc:** Near Church Stretton, this battle reputedly took place around AD 50 on the slopes and summit of this hill. It is believed that Caratacus, chieftain of the British Catuvellauni tribe, who after suffering a defeat in Kent at the hands of Aulus Plautius and his Roman army, fled to South Wales, there persuading the Silures tribe to rebel. He led them back to Shropshire to fight the Romans under Pubius Ostorius Scapula at the Battle of Caer Caradoc, which the Romans won. After this final defeat, Caratacus (Caradoc in Welsh) fled into the lands of the Brigantes tribe, who were loyal to Rome. He was captured and handed over to the Romans by Queen Cartimandua, and transported to Rome, where he was sentenced to death. However, after hearing an eloquent speech made by Caractacus, the Emperor Claudius was persuaded to spare his life. The site of this battle is disputed; some claim that it took place in the Malvern Hills, others in Briedden.

**The Battle of Maserfield** near Oswestry was joined on 5 August AD 642 (some make the year 641) by two Anglo-Saxon kings. Oswald, King of Northumberland, a Christian, was defeated by the pagan Penda, King of Mercia and his Welsh ally, Cynddylan ap Cyndrwyn, King of Powys. After the battle, Penda ordered a sacrifice to the god Woden, and the head and limbs of his dead opponent were severed and hung on trees and stakes. Legend has it that a swooping eagle snatched up one arm and dropped it at Cae Nef (Heaven Field), where a spring miraculously burst forth from the ground – now known as St Oswald's Well. The traditional location for the battle is Oswestry, meaning Oswald's Tree (in Welsh, it's Croesoswallt, meaning Oswald's Cross). Oswald was subsequently venerated as a martyr and saint.

OSWALD'S WELL
OSWESTRY

## SHROPSHIRE AND THE NORMAN CONQUEST

As early as 1068–69, the Shropshire border locals united against their new common enemy – the Normans. Saxons from Shropshire and Cheshire under Lord Edric allied with the Welsh and rose up against their Norman oppressors, winning several battles and laying siege to Shrewsbury and Hereford. It took the intercession of William the Conqueror himself before the rebellion was successfully put down (see Edric the Wild in People).

It wasn't just the Normans versus the Saxons and the Welsh. No, the Normans themselves proved to be a disagreeable lot. Many of King William I's supporters were unhappy with the distribution of the spoils, and disputed the line of succession when William died. Many Norman lords openly revolted against the choice of William Rufus (William II), who ruled England for almost three years. They revolted again after Rufus's death, when his brother, the conqueror's youngest son Henry (Henry I), was named as Rufus's successor. William I's eldest son, Robert Curthose, Duke of Normandy, was not content with his lot, and invaded England in an attempt to depose his younger brother. One of Curthose's main supporters was Robert de Bellême, 3rd Earl of Shrewsbury. In 1101, he fortified Bridgnorth Castle, a year before Robert Curthose made his challenge for the throne of England. King Henry I successfully besieged Robert de Bellême's castles at Bridgnorth and Shrewsbury, thus securing his rule. Robert de Bellême was stripped of his title as Earl of Shrewsbury, which was not used again for over 200 years.

A couple of decades later, in the 1100s, during the reign of King Stephen, Shropshire was again at the heart of a rebellion against the crown. This time it was the hard-done-by barons who revolted. In 1135, Stephen had seized the throne after successfully opposing Henry I's daughter Matilda's rightful claim, splitting the country in the process. Shrewsbury, Bridgnorth, Ludlow, Ellesmere and Whittington all supported Matilda, but in 1139, King Stephen and his army swept into Shropshire determined to teach the rebellious barons a swift lesson. Shrewsbury Castle was successfully stormed, and close to 100 of its garrison were reportedly hanged in reprisal. Ludlow Castle was also besieged, but held out. It is said that during the siege, the young Prince of Scotland, one of the king's allies, was caught by a grappling iron thrown by the defenders of the Beacon Tower. King Stephen hurried to free the prince before the defenders could get their hands on him. Many of the rebel Shropshire barons managed to hold out against Stephen, and in the end a truce was negotiated.

In 1155, the Shropshire lord Hugh de Mortimer, who had castles at Cleobury and Bridgnorth, was not happy with the new king, Henry II, who came to the throne in 1154, and he rebelled openly. The king moved into the county with a strong army, capturing both of Hugh's castles. Cleobury was razed to the ground, but Bridgnorth fared better, becoming a royal stronghold. It is believed that Pan Pudding Hill was used as a siege castle by the king during his attack on Bridgnorth Castle.

The Welsh had been quiet for a time, but in 1195, commanded by Prince Rhys, they stormed and burnt the timber-built castle at Clun. This is probably why stone was used when it was rebuilt.

When in 1199 John Lackland (King John) succeeded his brother Richard the Lionheart, trouble on the border flared up again. King John was not a popular monarch and his seventeen-year reign was packed with internal conflict, much of it coming from the Shropshire barons. Nor were the Welsh about to give the king an easy ride, despite John marrying off his illegitimate daughter to Prince Llewellyn of Wales. In Shropshire, King John besieged the castles at Clun and Oswestry, which at that time were held by the Fitz-Alan family.

Prince Llewellyn led Welsh attacks on Shrewsbury Castle in 1215 and again in 1234, capturing the castle both times. In 1223, the Welsh captured the partly built Whittington Castle – the curtain wall and towers of the inner bailey had still to be completed.

In response to an increased threat from Wales between 1250 and 1260, King Henry III ordered the strengthening of many castles in Shropshire. Once again, there was a power struggle between the king and the Shropshire lords, resulting in the capture of Ellesmere by the rebel barons. In the summer of 1263, Bishop's Castle was stormed, and occupied for sixteen weeks by John Fitz-Alan, killing a constable in the process.

When King Edward I came to the throne in 1272, he decided that enough was enough, and set about subduing the Welsh once and for all. By 1277, his conquest of Wales was complete, or so he thought. Edward's campaign should have made Shropshire safe from Welsh attack, but unfortunately no one told the Welsh, who rose up again in 1282, destroying Rowton Castle in their rampage.

One year later, in 1283, the English finally caught up with David ap Gruffyd, the Prince of Wales, and he was executed at Shrewsbury for treason against King Edward.

All was reasonably quiet on the English–Welsh border until the early 1400s, when Owain Glyn Dwr (Owen Glendower) came on the scene. In 1402, he led his Welsh army to victory at the Battle of Bry Glas on the River Lugg, south-west of Knighton, defeating Sir Edmund Mortimer. In 1404, Glyn Dwr was crowned Prince of Wales. In 1410, he led another revolt against King Henry IV, during which the castles at Clun, Oswestry and Whittington were all attacked. After 1414 nothing more was heard of this Welsh prince.

**The Battle of Shrewsbury, 21 July 1403:** Miffed that King Henry IV had failed to reward his family for securing the northern border country, Sir Henry 'Harry Hotspur' Percy's resentment grew into full rebellion. The king in question was of course that noted usurper Henry Bolingbroke or Henry IV, cousin of King Richard II, who in 1399 had deposed and imprisoned the king with the full support of the Percy family, most notably from Hotspur's father, Henry Percy, 1st Earl of Northumberland. In 1403, the Percys demanded that the king repay a debt of £20,000, a demand that fell on deaf ears. Hotspur himself had been given high office in Wales by the king, but he too had not been paid. The Percys also accused King Henry of starving Richard II to death in his castle at Pontefract. This and other disagreements forced Hotspur into an alliance with his brother-in-law Edward Mortimer and the Welsh patriot Owain Glyn Dwr, who was Mortimer's son-in-law. Feeling safe in this alliance, Hotspur hatched a scheme to divide England, and in July 1403 he headed south with 160 followers, bound for Shrewsbury to join forces with Glyn Dwr. By 19 July, his army, which included George, Earl Douglas, had swelled to around 14,000 strong. At that time, Shrewsbury was garrisoned for the king. When the news reached King Henry, he raced westwards with his army, succeeding in intercepting Hotspur before he could join forces with the Welsh, cornering him near Harlscott, 3 miles north of Shrewsbury. On 21 July, the two armies faced each other, and when negotiations failed, a couple of hours before dusk, the king's troops advanced. They were met by a deluge of arrows from Hotspur's Cheshire archers, but pressed on. Bloody hand-to-hand fighting followed, during which Harry Hotspur was killed, and by dusk the rebels had fled the field.

Shrewsbury was the first major battle in which English archers had fought against each other on their own soil, and provided a brutal lesson in the effectiveness of the longbow in the hands of skilled exponents, which Henry V would use so effectively at the Battle of Agincourt in 1415. The Battle of Shrewsbury ended the Percy family's challenge to Henry IV.

The church on the battlefield was established as a memorial to the dead in 1409. The site is now run by English Heritage. It is widely believed that Owain Glyn Dwr's ability to launch a sustained revolt was considerably reduced by the loss of his many potential allies at the Battle of Shrewsbury. The full story, or rather Shakespeare's version of it, can be found in *Henry IV, Part 1*.

**Shropshire and the Wars of the Roses, 1455–85:** The Wars of the Roses pitted the houses of Lancaster and York against each other for control of England. Shropshire was divided in its support, most of the land in the Welsh Marches being attached to the Duchy of York. The Duchy of Lancaster lands were mainly in Gloucestershire, North Wales and Cheshire.

Lancastrian King Henry VI, son of Henry V, was a pious, ineffectual and weak ruler who often lapsed into madness. He was also dominated by his avaricious wife Margaret of Anjou. Richard Plantagenet, Duke of York, was named Lord Protector of England, but many Lancastrians openly rejected him, and hostilities ensued. The first battle of the conflict was the First Battle of St Albans in 1455, which was won by King Henry VI. Following this, an uneasy peace pervaded the country until in 1459 Richard of York openly claimed the throne, renewing the conflict.

**The Battle of Blore Heath, 23 September 1459:** Although just a smidge across the Shropshire border in Staffordshire, this battle is worth a mention (Blore Heath lies 2 miles east of Market Drayton).

In early autumn the two sides found themselves in conflict. King Henry IV was raising troops in the Midlands; his queen, Margaret of Anjou, was in Cheshire. The main Lancastrian army, a force of around 10,000 men, commanded by Lord Audley, assisted by John, Lord Dudley, was at Market Drayton. On the queen's orders, Audley marched his army to intercept Richard Neville, the Earl of Salisbury, who was en route to Ludlow from Yorkshire with a Yorkist army of approximately 5,000 to join forces with Richard, Duke of York. The two armies met at Blore Heath. Salisbury positioned his inferior force on a small rise above a boggy depression and waited for the Lancastrians to attack. Lord Audley was seemingly unaware of the marshy conditions his men were advancing into, and of course the Lancastrian charge was hampered by the conditions underfoot. The Lancastrians who made it across the valley were cut to ribbons by the Yorkists. Lord Audley was killed, reputedly slain by Sir Roger Kynaston (father of the highwayman Humphrey Kynaston).

**The Sacking of Wem, 1459:** Following the Battle of Blore Heath, on his way to Ludlow the Earl of Salisbury took time out at the (Lancastrian) town of Wem to tear down its castle and town walls, also tearing down the church of St Peter and St Paul.

**The Battle of Ludford Bridge, 12 October 1459:** After winning the Battle of Blore Heath, and giving Wem a tonking, the Earl of Salisbury led his Yorkist forces to Ludlow, where he joined up with Richard, Duke of York, and the Earl of Warwick. The plan was to move to Worcester and thence to London. When they encountered a much larger Lancastrian force led by Henry VI, the Yorkists quickly fell back to Ludford Bridge. On the night of 11 October, 600 troops of the Yorkist army under Anthony Trollope, Captain of Calais, switched sides after accepting the king's pardon. On hearing of Trollope's desertion, York, Warwick and Salisbury crossed the bridge into the town, citing a need for refreshment, but instead abandoned their army and fled, leaving their leaderless men to face the music. The Duke of York fled into Wales with his son Edmund, Earl of Rutland. Salisbury, Warwick and York's son Edward, Earl of March (later King Edward VI), managed to reach the West Country, where Sir John Dynham provided a boat to take the fugitives to Calais. This Lancastrian walkover resulted in minimal casualties for at dawn on 13 October, the leaderless Yorkist army had no choice but to kneel in submission before King Henry, who graciously pardoned them. As was later discovered, Richard of York had not only abandoned his men, but also his wife, Cicely Neville, Duchess of York, and with her his two younger sons, George and Richard (later Richard III), plus his daughter Anne, whom the Lancastrians found standing at the Market Cross in Ludlow. They were placed in the care of the Duchess of York's sister Anne, wife of Lancastrian Humphrey Stafford, 1st Duke of Buckingham.

Sadly for Ludlow, the Lancastrian army proceeded to plunder the town, committing many outrages and drunken acts.

**The Battle of Mortimer's Cross, 2 February 1461:** This battle of the Roses was fought somewhere between Mortimer's Cross and the village of Kingsland in Shropshire. A Yorkist army commanded by Edward, Earl of March intercepted and defeated a Lancastrian force on its way from South Wales. In command was Jasper Tudor, Earl of Pembroke (King Henry VI's half-brother). After this Yorkist victory a number of Lancastrians, including Jasper's father, Owen Tudor, were captured and later executed at Hereford.

**Wem 1483:** The Duke of Buckingham had been well rewarded with high office and rich estates for helping Richard III take the throne. It was around this time that Richard's nephew, Edward V of England, and his younger brother, Richard of Shrewsbury, Duke of York (the Princes in the Tower), seemingly disappeared. What happened to them is not known for certain, nor is who, if anyone, murdered them. Both Richard III and the Duke of Buckingham have had the finger of suspicion pointed at them. Weeks after Richard's coronation, there was a failed plot to rescue the two boys from the Tower of London by starting fires in the city. Four men were executed for this and Buckingham suddenly changed sides, now supporting the Lancastrian cause. In October 1483 he invited Henry Tudor, Earl of Richmond, who was in exile abroad, to return to England to become king. Buckingham's motives for switching sides may never be known. One theory is that he murdered the princes to clear the way for his own attempt to take the throne, and that he planned Richard's death. Other theories are that his family were Lancastrians at heart and took the chance to demonstrate it. Either way, Buckingham's plans went up in smoke and he was forced to flee for his life, seeking shelter in Wem at the home of Ralph Bannister, one of his own retainers. Unfortunately, Bannister proved to be as disloyal as his liege lord and betrayed him. Buckingham was apprehended and taken to Shrewsbury. From there he was transferred to Salisbury, and beheaded on All Souls' Day, 2 November 1483.

## SHROPSHIRE AND THE ENGLISH CIVIL WAR

A number of Shropshire castles were garrisoned between King Charles and Parliament during the Civil War of the 1640s, despite many being in ruins. Eventually all the main Royalist strongholds were captured by the summer of 1646, although Bridgnorth held out until April, and Ludlow until June. The effects of the Civil War can be seen quite clearly at Bridgnorth: the leaning keep is a direct result of the castle being undermined and blown up by Parliamentarian forces following the 1646 siege.

In 1642, King Charles I raised his standard at Wellington. From there he moved his flag to Shrewsbury, where he was joined by his sons Charles and James, and Prince Rupert. He remained in Shrewsbury until 12 October, then marched to Bridgnorth, and from there to Edge Hill for the opening battle of the Civil War.

**Wem, 11 September 1643:** Here the Royalist stronghold of Wem was seized by a Parliamentarian force led by Sir Thomas Myddleton of Chirk, and General Thomas Mytton of Halston, who established the first Parliamentarian garrison there.

In October 1643, General Mytton defeated Lord Capel's attempt to retake the town.

**Ellesmere, 12 January 1644:** General Mytton surprised the Royalist defenders at Ellesmere, capturing ammunition together with Sir Nicholas Byron and Sir Richard Willis.

**The Siege at Hopton Castle:** Hopton Castle (owned by the Puritan Wallop family) in the village of Hopton, situated roughly half-way between Knighton and Craven Arms, was the scene of one of the bloodiest episodes in English history. In 1644 a 500-strong horse-and-foot unit of Prince Rupert's Royalist army laid siege to the castle under the command of Sir Michael Woodhouse. The defending Parliamentarian garrison under Samuel More numbered only around thirty Roundheads. After three weeks, seeing no alternative, More agreed terms and surrendered to the Cavalier force on 13 March. What happened next has been the subject of debate. Samuel More's own account is that only he of the defenders was spared, all the others being killed and buried. Other accounts hold that More held off surrendering until after the besiegers had captured the bailey, by which time the gateway to the keep was ablaze. In accordance with contemporary rules of war, Sir Michael Woodhouse decided against granting quarter, and so the majority of the defenders were killed. One account has it that the defenders' throats were cut and their bodies thrown into the moat. The castle was still habitable in 1700, but, like many others, soon fell into disrepair. The partially restored castle was the subject of a *Time Team* programme in 2010, and is now open to the public.

**The Siege of Oswestry, 22 June 1644:** Despite its glorious title, this Civil War siege lasted only a few hours. The town's castle and walls had been allowed to steadily decline over time to such an extent that their defence was nigh on impossible. The Royalist garrison consisted of twenty gentlemen of Shropshire and Wales plus around 200 officers and men. But by noon on 22 June the Parliamentarians under the Earl of Denbigh had captured St Oswald's church, and the following morning the Royalists surrendered. On Saturday 29 June, Colonel Marrow led a Royalist counter-attack involving fierce hand-to-hand fighting in the town that lasted three days. The church was recaptured, but not the castle. A relief Parliamentary force under Sir Thomas Myddleton was marching from Knutsford, which the Royalists were forced to meet in open battle at Felton Heath on 2 August: the Parliamentarians triumphed. Oswestry Castle was rendered unserviceable by the Parliamentarians over the next few years.

**Apley House, near Bridgnorth:** This was taken by Parliamentary forces under Sir John Price in February 1645, when sixty Royalist prisoners were captured, including Sir William Whitmore, Sir Thomas Whitmore and Sir Francis Oatley.

**Shrewsbury:** On 9 February 1645, the Royalist garrison was surprised by Sir Thomas Mytton. The town's governor, Sir Michael Earnly, was killed, and sixty gentlemen and 200 soldiers taken prisoner. Shrewsbury was finally captured by Parliamentary forces on 23 February 1645.

**Stokesay Castle, 10 June 1645:** Here the Royalist garrison was defeated and Sir William Croft was slain.

STOKESAY CASTLE

**High Ercall:** On 4 and 5 July 1645, Royalist Sir William Vaughan led his force to two victories over the Parliamentarian besiegers, and the garrison was relieved.

In August 1645, a Parliamentarian pamphlet was published listing all the castles garrisoned by the Royalists. The list included the castles at Bridgnorth, Broncroft, Caus, Dawley, Lee, Ludlow, Moreton Corbet, Oswestry, Rowton, Shrawardine, Stokesay and Tong. It is interesting that a number of fortified manor houses are included in this list, even though their defensive strength was limited, and certainly not strong enough to resist canon fire.

**The Siege of Bridgnorth, February/March 1646:** After a month-long siege, the Royalist garrison surrendered to the Parliamentarians (see Castles and Fortifications).

**High Ercall:** On 28 February 1646, the Royalist garrison under the command of Sir Vincent Corbet capitulated.

**Ludlow Castle:** On 9 July 1646, the Royalist garrison surrendered to Sir William Brereton (see Castles and Fortifications).

In 1651, following defeat at the Battle of Worcester, Charles II and the Earl of Derby escaped and travelled north. On 4 September they arrived at White Ladies Priory, where they received shelter before moving on to Boscobel House, where the king was forced to hide in an oak tree. From there they moved to Moseley Old Hall, just over the Shropshire border in Staffordshire (see Royal Shropshire).

On 15 October 1651, Colonel John Benbow, uncle of the famous admiral, was shot on Shrewsbury Castle Green.

In 1654, in an abortive Royalist uprising, Sir Thomas Harries made a surprise attack on Shrewsbury Castle, but his attempt failed.

From the mid-seventeenth century, the fate of the castle as a defensive structure was sealed. In order to prevent castles being used by Royalist supporters against Lord Protector Oliver Cromwell, many castles were slighted or destroyed.

# 13

# PEOPLE

## THE FAMOUS AND THE NOT SO FAMOUS

**Richard Baxter, 1615–91:** Puritan theologian and nonconformist, Richard Baxter was born in Rowton, baptised at High Ercall and grew up in Eaton Constantine. John Owen, of Wroxeter's free school, was an early tutor of his. Despite excelling in Latin, the teenaged Baxter declined to go to Oxford, choosing to continue his education at Ludlow Castle under Chaplain Richard Wickstead. Following a brief spell at court, he returned home to study divinity. He taught at Dudley Grammar School in 1638, before moving to Bridgnorth. His interest in nonconformity grew to such an extent that he was alienated from the Church of England. He stayed at Bridgnorth for almost two years. Then, in 1641, he moved to Kidderminster, where he was elected minister of St Mary and All Saints' church, where he stayed over eighteen years, moving to Gloucester when the Civil War began. He was preaching in Alcester near Stratford when the Battle of Edge Hill started. When he returned to Kidderminster he was driven out, moving to the Parliamentary stronghold of Coventry as chaplain to the garrison. Then, following the Battle of Naseby, he became chaplain to Colonel Walley's regiment until February 1647. Oliver Cromwell had earlier asked him to become chaplain to the Ironsides; he had declined, which Cromwell took badly, and henceforth avoided him. In May 1685, Baxter spent time in King's Bench Prison, charged with libelling the Church, and was brought up in front of Chief Justice Sir George Jeffreys, better known as the 'hanging judge'. He was sentenced to remain in prison until he paid a fine of 500 marks. Baxter's incarceration lasted eighteen months before the government remitted the fine. Baxter was now over 70 years old and in ill health, and spent the remainder of his life in peace. He passed away in 1691.

**Admiral John Benbow, 1653–1702:** The exact date of birth and the birthplace of future Royal Navy officer John Benbow have been widely disputed. Some believe he was born on 10 March 1653 in Newport, Shropshire; others believe his birthplace to have been Coton Hill, Shrewsbury. His parents were William and Martha Benbow. Members of Benbow's wider family included a namesake who had been a clerk to the Chancery who had been granted arms in 1584, and another John Benbow who had served as a captain in the Parliamentarian army and been shot on Shrewsbury Castle Green on 15 October 1651.

After attending the free school in Shrewsbury, John Benbow was apprenticed to a River Severn waterman and subsequently joined the Royal Navy, rising to the rank of admiral, achieving fame fighting the French during the War of Spanish Succession (1701–14). In August 1702 a number of captains under his command refused to support his decisions. He got the offenders back by instigating their trial, but died in Jamaica before they were punished.

Benbow became a popular figure and his exploits were often celebrated in song. In Robert Louis Stevenson's *Treasure Island*, Jim Hawkins's mother's inn is the Admiral Benbow. During an engagement with the French off Santa Marta, Benbow lost a leg, which proved fatal but ensured his place in the list of British naval heroes. The inscription on Benbow's tomb states that he was 52 when he died in 1702.

**Dr William Penny Brookes, 1809–96:** Dr Brookes was born in Much Wenlock, and is best known as the man responsible for the rebirth of the Olympic Games. An impressive figure with long whiskers and a strict expression, Brookes was convinced that the health of the town's population, particularly the working men, would be greatly improved through exercise; in his view, most workmen drank far too much. Brookes started exercise classes in 1850. Ten years later this developed into the Wenlock Olympian Society, which still exists. The Much Wenlock Olympian Games began in 1861 and comprised such diverse activities as putting the stone (shot-put), jumping, cricket, quoits, wheelbarrow races and a penny-farthing bicycle race over a 3-mile course. The local children also got to have a go at events including reading, spelling, history and, wait for it, knitting! Dr Brookes died at 87 in 1896, just a few months before the first modern International Olympic Games were held in April that year.

**Robert Burnell, 1239–92:** Born in Acton Burnell on 25 October 1239, Burnell rose to become Bishop of Bath and Wells, and Lord Chancellor of England to King Edward I, serving among his chief ministers and advisors. He is responsible for building the fortified manor house of Acton Burnell Castle and most of the village, including St Mary's church. Parliament Barn at Acton Burnell is so called because it was there that King Edward held the first-ever parliament where the commons were fully represented in the autumn of 1283. Burnell died in Berwick; his body is buried in Wells Cathedral, but his heart is buried in Bath Abbey.

**Robert Clive, 1725–74:** Clive of India was born 29 September at Styche Manor near Market Drayton, the son of lawyer Richard Clive. Robert Clive is best known for his time in India with the East India Company, and particularly for his spectacular military victories. He achieved rapid promotion after capturing the fort and port at Arcot in 1751, and repeating the feat at Madras. He followed up with a famous victory at Plassey against overwhelming odds.

He returned to England a hero in 1760, becoming MP for Shrewsbury, and was rewarded with an Irish peerage. He went back to India to sort out corruption and bribery scandals, then returned to England in 1767, this time not as a hero for his many jealous enemies had blackened his reputation. Over the next few years he was vilified by the same press that had previously hailed him a hero. MPs demanded an enquiry into Clive's enormous wealth, said to be almost £250,000. Robert Clive died on 22 November 1774 in his house in London's Berkeley Square, a broken man. The exact manner of his death is not clear. One rumour suggests that he slit his own throat; another is that he shot himself. His family claimed he died from an overdose of opium. Which is true? Who knows? Maybe we never will. We do know, however, that Clive had previously made two unsuccessful attempts at suicide as a young man in India, but on both occasions the pistol failed to fire.

**Charles Robert Darwin, 1809–82:** Shrewsbury's most venerated son, Charles Darwin was born 12 February 1809 at 'The Mount' (now known as 'Darwin House'), which is situated in the Frankwell area of the town. He was educated at Shrewsbury School, and then attended Edinburgh University with plans for a career in medicine. From there he studied at Christ's College, Cambridge. Among his relatives were Erasmus Darwin (his paternal grandfather), the noted scientist and poet, and Josiah Wedgwood (his maternal grandfather), the prominent pottery manufacturer.

In December 1821, when he was 22, Darwin signed up as naturalist on the surveying expedition on HMS *Beagle*, little realising how this epic five-year voyage would change his life. The expedition took in the Cape Verde Islands and other Atlantic islands, South America and most famously the Galapagos Islands. It also visited Tahiti, New Zealand, Australia, Tasmania, Keeling Island, the Maldives, Mauritius, St Helena, Ascension Island and Brazil, before ending in October 1836. Over the next twenty-plus years Darwin formulated and developed his theories of evolution, delaying their publication until 1859. *The Origin of Species*, expounding evolution through means of natural selection, caused an uproar and split the scientific community. The Church of England called it heresy.

Charles Darwin's theory entirely changed our understanding of history of animal life, particularly that of the human species. His forward-thinking book is one of the most important ever written. Shrewsbury celebrates its most famous son every February with the annual Darwin Festival.

**Henry Hill Hickman, 1800–30:** Henry Hill Hickman was born into a family of tenant farmers on 27 January 1800 at Lady Halton near Bromfield, just outside Ludlow. Aged 16, he began training in medicine in Edinburgh, and four years later became a member of the London Royal College of Surgeons. He set up practice in Ludlow in 1821, and in 1823 began searching for a way to achieve anaesthesia by cutting up animals he asphyxiated with carbon dioxide. He wrote his treatise in 1824 whilst living in Shifnal, and sent it to the President of the London Horticultural Society, Thomas Andrew Knight of Downton Castle, near Ludlow, hoping that it would be forwarded to Sir Humphrey Davy, the President of the Royal Society. Receiving no support for his theories in England, in 1828 he turned to the French king, again without success. On his return to England, he set up his practice in Tenbury Wells, but a year later he died, possibly of tuberculosis. Hickman is lauded today as a pioneer of anaesthesia, the science that saves mankind from pain.

**Lord Rowland Hill, 1772–1842:** Rowland Hill was born near Hawkstone on 11 August 1772, rising to become one of Shropshire's most famous soldiers. Known to his men as 'Daddy Hill', he was educated in Chester. He was commissioned into the 38th Regiment of Foot in 1790, and thence to the 53rd Foot in 1791, seeing service at the Siege of Toulon in 1793, and then with the 90th Foot at Abu Qir Bay in Egypt, where he received a serious head wound from a musket ball. He was promoted brigadier in 1803, and major-general in 1805. Part of Wellington's army in the Peninsular War, Hill's troops were involved in the battles of Rolica and Vimiero, and subsequently at Corunna, Oporto, Talavera and Bussaco. Hill came down with malaria before the Battle of Albuera and was forced to hand command of his troops to Sir William Beresford. Recovered, Hill led a successful attack on the French at Arroyo dos Molinos. In February 1812 he was made a Knight of the Grand Order of Bath (KB). Hill was involved in the capture of Badajoz, and the victories at the battles of Almaraz, Vitoria, Pyrenees, Nivelle, Nive, Orthez and Toulouse. When peace with France came, he was appointed Governor of Hull in 1814, and was MP for Shrewsbury between 1812 and 1814. After Napoleon's escape from Elba, Hill commanded the 2nd Army Company at the Battle of Waterloo, leading a charge against Bonaparte's Imperial Guard, narrowly escaping death.

Hill's unstinting bravery and leadership earned him many honours both from home and from overseas, and in 1828 he was appointed Commander-in-Chief of the Forces, succeeding the Duke of Wellington, later becoming Governor of Plymouth and, in 1830, Viscount Hill of Almaraz. Lord Rowland Hill died at Hardwicke Grange, Hadnall, on 10 December 1842, and is buried in the churchyard at Hadnall church. His statue sits proudly on top of one of Shrewsbury's greatest landmarks, the Doric column adjacent to the offices of Shropshire County Council.

**Eglantyne Jebb, 1876–1928:** Born in Ellesmere on 25 August 1876, Eglantyne Jebb co-founded 'Save the Children' in 1919 to raise funds for famine-stricken children in Germany and Austria after the end of the First World War. Her draft for the 'Declaration of the Rights of the Child' was adopted by the League of Nations and an expanded version was adopted by the United Nations in 1959, inspiring the 1989 UN Convention on the Rights of the Child. She died on 17 December 1928 and her lasting legacy is a truly wonderful worldwide charity for children.

**Sir Humphrey Kynaston:** The sixteenth-century highwayman Humphrey Kynaston is Shropshire's very own Robin Hood. Although his birth date is unknown, we know that he died in 1534. The youngest son of the High Sheriff of Shropshire, Sir Roger Kynaston, Humphrey grew up in Myddle Castle, where he was oft in trouble, earning himself the nickname Wild Humphrey Kynaston. Following one of his escapades he was convicted of the murder of John Hughes of Stretton on 20 December 1491, and was subsequently outlawed by order of King Henry VII. To escape punishment Humphrey lived in a cave in the sandstone cliff of Nesscliffe Hill, from where, mounted on his famous horse Beelzebub, he embarked on a life of robbery, earning a reputation for robbing the rich and giving to the poor, a spree that lasted until 1518. He inherited Myddle Castle from his father, but allowed the estate to fall into disrepair. Humphrey appears to have been well loved by the local people, who fed him and his horse, and went out of their way to help him avoid capture.

One story goes that the sheriff, hoping to corner the outlaw and capture him, had several wooden planks removed from the surface of the Montford Bridge over the River Severn on Kynaston's route back to his hideout, but Beelzebub cleared the gap in one huge leap and the pair escaped.

Humphrey was married at least twice, fathering eight children, possibly more if indeed he married a third time, as another legend has it. It is claimed that Humphrey regularly patronised the Old Three Pigeons Tavern at Nesscliffe, and his seat can still be seen carved into the inglenook fireplace. There is talk of his ghost haunting the place, Beelzebub too. Some believe that in 1493 he received a pardon from the king; other accounts state that in 1513 he raised a force of 100 men to fight for Henry VIII, for which he received a royal pardon. Whichever is true, we know that he died in 1534 (his will is dated 1 May 1534), although the exact manner and place of his death remain a mystery.

**Frances Moore, 1657–1715:** Born to a poor family in Bridgnorth on 29 January 1657, Frances Moore taught himself to read and educated himself. He grew up to be a physician and astrologer, serving at the court of Charles II. Old Moore's almanac was published for the first time in 1699, including such things as predictions about the weather and astrological items. The almanac is still published today.

**John Mytton, 1796–1838:** Born 30 September 1796, John was just 2 years old when his father died. Inheriting a fortune, plus Halston Hall near Whittington and its estates, John (or Jack as he became known) grew up to become one of Shropshire's best-remembered sportsmen. He earned the nickname 'Mad Jack Mytton' for his madcap escapades. As he grew older, the young squire became much more eccentric, adding drunkenness to his many wanton excesses, reputedly getting through up to six bottles of port every day. He is said to have kept a menagerie of 2,000 dogs, and more than sixty finely costumed cats, plus a brown bear called Nell, which he rode around his dining room, until the day the bear bit him on the calf.

Renowned for his practical jokes, Jack Mytton devoted his life to horse racing, gambling, hunting, alcohol and daredevil escapades, often risking his life to pull off another dangerous feat. Stories of his death-defying stunts include galloping his horse across a rabbit warren to see what would happen, riding directly at the most dangerous obstacle he could espy and racing his four-horse gig along narrow country lanes at breakneck speeds, tearing round bends and across crossroads, once unsuccessfully attempting to jump the gig over a tollbooth – so little regard did he have for his own life.

His lack of any paternal guidance during his early years, coupled with the prospect of inherited wealth, no doubt caused John to turn out as he did. His education proved to be somewhat patchy; expelled from Westminster School for fighting the masters, he lasted only three days at Harrow. He then had to be tutored privately. When he got a place at Cambridge University, he reputedly ordered 2,000 bottles of port to keep him going while he studied, but before starting he changed his mind and embarked on a Grand Tour of Europe instead. After this he joined the 7th Hussars for a year before moving back to Halston Hall. On his twenty-first birthday he inherited £60,000, plus estates worth £18,000 per year. He purchased the seat as Member of Parliament for Shrewsbury, but soon found Westminster politics boring.

Mad Jack had a passion for horse racing. His colt Euphrates won the Gold Cup in 1825. Another of his favourite horses, called Sportsman, died after drinking a bowl of mulled port, but his favourite of all was a horse named Baronet, which Mytton gave the run of the house and allowed to lounge in front of the fire of Halston Hall. Once, returning from Doncaster Races in his carriage, Jack fell asleep whilst counting his money, and several thousand pounds worth of banknotes were blown out of the window to be scattered across the countryside. His first marriage, in 1818, ended less than two years later when his wife died. His second wife, Caroline Gifford, left him in 1830.

At the age of 38, and heavily in debt, in the seventeen years since his inheritance Mytton had spent something like £500,000. Jack abandoned his estates and fled to Calais with a woman he met on Westminster Bridge whom he paid £500 to accompany him, but it didn't last. In France one day his cure for hiccups turned out to be setting fire to his own shirt. Ill health forced him back to England in 1834, where he was arrested and committed to King's Bench Prison.

His extravagant lifestyle finally having caught up with him, and having lost both house and fortune, the once-wealthy squire of Halston Hall died in a debtor's prison. Nevertheless, such was his reputation for extreme generosity, that it is said more than 3,000 people turned out to mourn at his funeral.

His memory is marked by the Jack Mytton Way – a 93-mile (150km) footpath and bridleway, and in the name of the Mytton and Mermaid Hotel, plus a number of thoroughfares in Shropshire.

**Wilfred Edward Salter Owen, 1893–1918:** Widely regarded as the finest war poet of the twentieth century, Wilfred Owen was born in Plas Wilmot, Oswestry on 18 March 1893, the eldest of four children. His family later moved to Monkmoor in Shrewsbury. He was educated at Birkenhead Institute, and latterly at Shrewsbury Technical College, where his passion for poetry was originally influenced by the work of John Keats and Percy Shelley. Wilfred Owen enlisted in the Artists' Rifles Officers' Training Corps on 21 October 1915, undertaking seven months of training in Essex before being commissioned in to the Manchester Regiment as a second lieutenant. Sent to France in 1916, Owen saw action, was concussed after falling into a shell hole, and subsequently blown up by a trench mortar. Shell-shocked, he spent time in Craiglockhart War Hospital in Edinburgh, where he met poet Siegfried Sassoon, who also influenced Owen's poetry. Owen wrote some of his most popular verse during this period of recuperation. He returned to the trenches at the end of August 1918, leading units that stormed enemy positions near the French village of Joncourt, where his bravery in capturing a German machine gun post saw him awarded the Military Cross in October 1918. Owen's remarkably vivid poetry told the truth about the horrors of war and trench warfare and shocked people with its reality. He tragically died at Ors, aged 25, on 4 November 1918, during a battle crossing the Sambre-Oise Canal, one week before the end of the Great War. There is a memorial to him in the grounds of Shrewsbury Abbey, and of course his poetry lives on.

**Ellis Peters, more properly Edith Mary Pargeter, OBE, BEM, 1913–95:** This popular writer was born in Horsehay on 28 September. Although she is best known for her Brother Cadfael novels, which were popularised on television with Derek Jacobi in the lead role,

Edith Pargeter also wrote many history books and other historical mysteries. She also wrote in a number of different styles, published under her real name and under various pen names besides Ellis Peters, among them John Redfern, Jolyon Carr and Peter Benedict. A fluent Czech speaker, she received honours for her translations of classic Czech stories. Edith was educated in Dawley and at Coalbrookdale Girls High School, and during the Second World War served in the Wrens. Many of her stories had a strong Welsh element. Edith Pargeter passed away aged 82 at her home in Madeley on 14 October 1995.

**Wild Edric or Eadric the Wild:** Saxon thane Edric Sylvaticus held large tracts of land within the ancient kingdom of Mercia (modern-day Shropshire and Staffordshire). Following the Battle of Hastings in 1066, he refused to swear allegiance to Duke William (King William I), and a year later began a war of attrition against the Norman invaders. Edric proved to be a wily opponent and, in alliance with Welsh princes, inflicted defeats on the local Norman commander and his forces. Edric and his army devastated Hereford and its new castle before things calmed down for a while, but in 1069 Edric was at it again, this time besieging Shrewsbury's castle and burning the town when he failed to capture it. On campaign in the north, King William was understandably irritated at the news, and marched his army south to put down the uprising. Edric and his rebels submitted to William and finally swore fealty. What happened to Edric is not known for certain. Tradition has it that he rebelled again only to be captured at Wigmore by Ralph de Mortimer, and died in prison. An alternative account has him escaping and living out his life in Wales.

**Len Murray, 1922–2004:** Born in Hadley, Telford on 2 August 1922, Lionel 'Len' Murray, Baron Murray of Epping Forest, OBE, PC, is best known as the General Secretary of the TUC. After studying English at the University of London, he was commissioned into the King's Shropshire Light Infantry (KSLI) and was badly wounded in Normandy. Len Murray died in hospital of emphysema and pneumonia on 20 May 2004.

**John Gwynn, 1713–86:** Shrewsbury-born architect and civil engineer, and founder member of the Royal Academy in 1768. Builder of the English Bridge in Shrewsbury in 1769, Atcham's Old Bridge in

ÁTCHÁM OLD BRIDGE

1769–71, Magdalen Bridge in Oxford in 1772–90 and another in Worcester in 1781. He died in Shrewsbury on 28 February 1786.

**Richard Legg:** Famous for the production of clay pipes in Broseley. The 'Churchwarden Pipe' was 25in long.

**Dr William Withering, 1741–99:** This Wellington-born physician and botanist wrote *An Account of the Foxglove and some of its Medical Uses; with practical remarks on the dropsy, and some other diseases* (1785). This introduced digitalis as a drug for cardiac disease, remembering the unknown market woman who sold him some medicine she had made from foxgloves (*digitalis purpurea*).

## A FEW FAMOUS PEOPLE ASSOCIATED WITH SHROPSHIRE

**Abraham Darby I, 1678–1717:** Born in Wren's Nest, Woosetton, near Dudley on 14 April 1678, Abraham Darby was the first of three successive generations to bear the same name. Each played a pivotal role in the Industrial Revolution. His father was yeoman John Darby, a locksmith and farmer by trade and his mother was Ann Baylies. Darby could count nobility amongst his forebears, albeit from the wrong side of the blanket – his great-grandmother was an illegitimate daughter of Edward Sutton, 5th Baron Dudley, and her brother, metallurgist Dud Dudley, was one of the first Englishmen to smelt iron using coke as a fuel instead of expensive charcoal. Perhaps it was Dud's work that inspired his great-grandnephew Abraham Darby in his quest to perfect this method of economical smelting. As a young man, Darby was apprenticed to Quaker Jonathan Freeth in Birmingham, a maker of brass grinding mills, and in 1699 he married Mary Sergeant, the couple setting up home in Bristol. At Coalbrookdale in 1709, Darby successfully smelted pig iron in a coke-fired blast furnace, enabling the first large-scale production of cast-iron. Items made in Ironbridge were shipped all over the world.

Abraham Darby died in 1717 aged only 38, at his home at Madeley Court on the outskirts of Madeley, following an eighteen-month illness. He was buried in the Broseley Quaker burial ground; his wife died a few months later, leaving a young family. Darby's business was in a state so his shares were mortgaged. Help came from various sources in the family, including Mary's brother, Joshua Sergeant, who purchased shares on behalf of Darby's children.

These next three Abraham Darbys were actually born in Shropshire:

**Abraham Darby II, 1711–63:** Born in Coalbrookdale on 12 May 1711, Abraham II was only 6 when his father died. After completing his education in 1728, he began helping to manage the works at his father's company, and in 1732 was rewarded with four company shares. The Coalbrookdale Company now produced cast-iron goods of all kinds: kettles, cooking pots and iron cylinders for the steam engines of Thomas Newcome, which were much cheaper than brass. Like his father, he died at a relatively young age, 51, on 31 March 1763. He had three children from his first marriage, and six from his second, among them Abraham Darby III.

**Abraham Darby III, 1750–89:** Born in Coalbrookdale on 24 April 1750 and educated in Worcester, at the age of 13 Abraham III inherited his father's shares in the business. In 1768, at the tender age of 18, the young Darby took on the management of the ironworks at Coalbrookdale. A generous employer, Darby introduced many improvements to the conditions of his workers, including building houses, and paying higher wages than other industries. He also developed farms, where he grew food for his workforce and their families. He died at Madeley in 1789 and, like his father and grandfather, was at a young age: he was only 39. He left seven children and was buried in Coalbrookdale Quaker burial ground. His sons Francis and Richard carried on their father's work. It was during Abraham III's tenure, in 1779, that the world's first cast-iron bridge was built, spanning the River Severn using iron from Darby's factories. The bridge is beautifully constructed, very innovative, and today the Ironbridge stands as a permanent reminder of the innovation of our industrial past.

**Abraham Darby IV, 1804–78:** The fourth Abraham Darby was a great-nephew of Abraham Darby III. He was born 30 March 1804 at Dale House, Coalbrookdale. In 1830, with his brother Alfred, he took on the management of the Coalbrookdale Company's Horsehay foundry, investing in new processes to manufacture wrought iron. Fourteen years later he was a major shareholder in the ironworks at Ebbw Vale, South Wales, after resigning from the Coalbrook Company. He moved to Stoke Court near Stoke Poges, Buckinghamshire. He was a JP, and in 1853, became High Sheriff of Buckinghamshire. Although brought up a Quaker like his ancestors and the rest of his family, Abraham IV joined the Church of England, raising the money to build Coalbrookdale's Holy Trinity church, where he is buried. He died on 28 November 1878 in Treberfydd, Breconshire.

Back to those associated with the county:

**Alfred Edward Houseman, 1859–1936:** Houseman, usually known as A.E. Houseman, was born in Bromsgrove on 26 of March 1859. He was a classical scholar and poet best known for his lyrical cycle of sixty-three poems *A Shropshire Lad*, which he published at his own expense in May 1896. The work appealed to late Victorian, Edwardian and Georgian tastes, inspiring many English composers before and after the First World War. One of the foremost classic poets, and one of the greatest scholars of all time, Houseman was appointed Professor of Latin at UCL and subsequently at Cambridge. In 1911 he accepted the Kennedy Professorship of Latin at Trinity College, Cambridge, where he remained until he died.

*A Shropshire Lad* has been in print continuously since first published. A.E. Houseman died on 30 April 1936 in Cambridge. His ashes are buried near St Laurence's church in Ludlow, where there is a plaque dedicated to him.

**Judge Jeffreys, 1645–89:** Born at Acton Hall, Wrexham, George Jeffreys was closely associated with Shropshire. Educated at Shrewsbury School, he became Lord Chief Justice in 1683, Lord Chancellor in 1685, and was created a baron in 1685 and took the title of Lord Jeffreys of Wem – reputedly a place he never went to. He was the Lord Lieutenant of Shropshire from 1687 to 1689, but is most widely remembered as the 'Hanging Judge' for his conduct of the Bloody Assizes in September 1685 after the defeat of Monmouth's West Country rebellion. His language from the bench was often violent and sarcastic, and he was only saved from the fury of a mob (following the flight of his master, King James II) by his imprisonment in the Tower, where he died shortly afterwards.

**Thomas Telford, 1757–1834:** Renowned in his day as the 'Colossus of Roads', Thomas Telford was born 9 August 1757 in Westerkirk, Scotland. He travelled to Shrewsbury to restore MP Earl Pulteney's house, converting the derelict ruin of Shrewsbury Castle into a home. The folly Laura's Tower (still seen within the grounds) was built for the MP's wife. He stayed on to become Surveyor of Public Works in 1787, and among his other projects were Shrewsbury Prison, Bridgnorth's St Mary Magdalene church and St Michael's church in Madeley. In 1788, Telford carried out the first excavations at the site of Wroxeter Roman City, and two years later he designed the Montford Bridge near Shrewsbury, to carry the London–Holyhead road over the River Severn. This was the first of forty bridges he built in Shropshire, including Buildwas Bridge, Telford's first iron bridge, strongly influenced by the iron bridge in Ironbridge. Another of his bridges at Cound spans the River Tern and is preserved as a scheduled ancient monument. Three of Telford's other notable bridges are at Bridgnorth, Bewdley and at Dinham, Ludlow (since replaced, though one of the original arches was incorporated into the new structure: the arch nearest to Ludlow town centre was part of

Telford's bridge). Telford's many achievements include the design of the cast-iron aqueduct at Longdon-on-Tern, substantially bigger than the UK's first cast-iron aqueduct, built by Benjamin Outram on the Derby Canal just months earlier.

In 1793, Telford was appointed to manage the design and construction of the Ellesmere Canal (now known as the Llangollen Canal), joining Ellesmere to the Chester Canal, thus linking the ironworks and collieries of Wrexham with Chester, and on to the River Mersey. This canal provided many engineering challenges, including the spectacular Pontcysyllte Aqueduct (the name means 'connecting bridge'). Here Telford used a new method of construction: cast-iron plate troughs fixed in masonry. The Ellesmere Canal was completed in 1805. An engineering marvel, the Pontcysyllte Aqueduct, known as 'the waterway in the sky', carries the Llangollen Canal 126ft over the River Dee in the Vale of Llangollen, taking in the beautiful scenery of North Shropshire. Telford's next project was the design and construction of the Shrewsbury Canal, after Joseph Clowes, the original engineer, died in 1795. The 17-mile canal was built with eleven locks, eight lift bridges and a 970yd tunnel at Berwick. This canal was finally abandoned in 1944, but some of the original bridges still remain. Between 1796 and 1801, Telford built the 70ft-tall Chirk Aqueduct over the River Ceiriog. The railway viaduct was added in 1846, standing 30ft above the canal. It is also special in that it is half in England and half in Wales. Following his successful aqueduct projects, Telford returned to Scotland to build the Caledonian Canal. But he did return to Shropshire for his greatest and most ambitious project: the Shropshire Union Canal, formerly known as the Birmingham and Liverpool Canal. This linked the Birmingham Canal network at Wolverhampton with the sea at Ellesmere Port, and with many small canals on its route. The Shropshire Union Canal, Telford's last, was still used for commercial traffic until 1958. In his later years, Telford was responsible for building many roads, notably the London to Holyhead Road (A5), specifically the 106-mile section between Shrewsbury and Holyhead. In 1820, Telford was appointed first president of the Institution of Civil Engineers, a post he held until his death on 2 September 1834. He died before the opening of the Shropshire Union Canal, and is buried in Westminster Abbey.

The modern town of Telford was named in his honour in 1968. More recently, Thomas Telford School in Telford, opened in 1990, is one of fourteen technology colleges named after the great man.

**Percy Thrower, MBE, 1913–88:** Although not a native of Shropshire, the name of Percy Thrower became synonymous with the county. Born 30 January 1913 at Horwood House in Little Horwood, Buckinghamshire, Thrower's desire was to follow in his father's footsteps and become a head gardener. He worked in Windsor Castle's royal gardens, and for the Parks Department in Derby, before coming to Shrewsbury. In 1946, at 32 years of age, Thrower was promoted to the post of Shrewsbury Parks Superintendent, a job he kept until he retired in 1974. In the early 1950s, Percy Thrower was a regular on BBC radio's *Beyond the Back Door*, and then on BBC television, appearing on such shows as *Country Calender*, *Out and About*, *Gardener's World* and *Blue Peter*, winning the hearts of the British people. Along the riverside at Shrewsbury is Percy Thrower's masterpiece – The Dingle: a marvellous sunken garden packed with arrays of flowers and plants around an enchanting centre of water features. His Percy Thrower Garden Centre at Meole Brace in Shrewsbury is still thriving. In 1977, Thrower was awarded the Victoria Medal of Honour, the Royal Horticultural Society's highest honour, and in 1984 he was awarded the MBE. Percy Thrower, television's first celebrity gardener, died on 18 March 1988.

# 14

# LITERARY SHROPSHIRE

## OF BOOKS AND WRITERS

**William Shakespeare** makes many a mention of Shrewsbury in his play *Henry IV*, which of course includes the Battle of Shrewsbury.

In Act IV, Scene II, Sir John Falstaff asks: 'What, Hal? How now, mad way? What a devil dost thou in Warwickshire? My good Lord of Westmorland, I cry you mercy. I thought your honour had already been at Shrewsbury.' Then, in Act V, Scene IV, he boasts that he and Hotspur had 'fought a long hour by Shrewsbury clock' – possibly referring to St Mary's clock or the clock on the old Market Hall in the square, though he must have been blessed with fantastic eyesight to see either from the site of the battlefield. The play also includes the line, spoken by King Henry IV, 'How bloodily the sun begins to peer. Above yon busky hill the day looks pale,' possibly referring to Haughmond Hill. In Act III, Scene II, the same play includes two references to Bridgnorth (but spelt with an e in the middle).

**Charles Dickens** (1812–70) has many connections to the county of Shropshire. The closing chapters of *The Old Curiosity Shop* are reputed to have been set in the graveyard of Tong church, where lies the grave of 'Little Nell'. And lo and behold, such a grave appeared. This followed the serialisation of the story, which was then successfully published in the USA, its popularity so enormous that American visitors to Shropshire wanted to see the grave for themselves. Not wanting to miss out on the profits of tourism, the residents of Tong contributed to a fund to pay for a headstone – and thus everyone was happy. It is suggested that Dickens visited Tong when his grandmother worked at Tong Castle (see Castles and Fortifications).

**John Betjemen**'s 1940 poem 'A Shropshire Lad', not to be confused with the work of A.E. Houseman, commemorates the death of the famous swimmer Captain Matthew Webb.

**A.E. Houseman** of course wrote wonderfully of Clunton, Clunbury, Clungunford and Clun.

Romantic historical novelist **Sir Walter Scott** is believed to have stayed in Clun while writing *The Betrothed* and *The Talisman*, published jointly on 22 June 1825, under the title of *Tales of the Crusaders*. It's thought that he stayed at the Buffalo Inn, and that he used Clun Castle as his inspiration for the fortress Garde Douleureuse.

**Bruce Chatwin** penned *On the Black Hill* during a stay at Cwm Hall, near Craven Arms.

**E.M. Forster** visited Clun, and subsequently used the town as the model for Oniton in *Howards End*.

**Douglas Adams** mentions Clun in *The Meaning of Liff*, cruelly listing it as a 'leg that has gone to sleep that you have to drag around behind you'.

In 1878 a young Scottish medical student, **Arthur Conan Doyle**, worked for four months as an unpaid assistant to Dr Eliot in Ruyton village, living at Cliffe House. The renowned author of the Sherlock Holmes adventures later recalled Ruyton in his *Memories and Recollections*, published in 1923, as 'not big enough to make one town, far less eleven'. Conan Doyle's connection with Shropshire is more than just a stay in Ruyton – he also wrote a short melodramatic piece for *Chambers's Journal* about a murder, 'The Bravoes of Market Drayton' (see Shropshire Murders).

Children's author **Malcolm Saville** (1901–82), though born in Sussex, developed a special affinity with Shropshire after he, his wife and four children were evacuated to the county during the Second World War. He wrote over ninety books, both fiction and non-fiction, many featuring Shropshire, such as the 'Lone Pine Club' adventures, which are set in and around Clun, and the first 'Buckingham' adventures.

**Samuel Taylor Coleridge**, author of the poem 'The Rime of the Ancient Mariner', briefly ministered as locum to Dr Rowe, the Unitarian minister at his church in Shrewsbury's High Street.

*Comus* by **John Milton** was first performed in the Great Hall at Ludlow Castle in 1634. The play was set in the local woods and the children of the Lord President of the Council of the Marches, John Egerton, Earl of Bridgwater, were cast as themselves.

# ACTORS

**Peter Vaughan:** Peter Ewart Olm was born in Wem on 4 April 1923, later adopting the stage name Vaughan. A familiar name to television viewers, Peter is best known for playing the part of Grouty, the jailed crime boss in Ronnie Barker's *Porridge*, and his role in *Citizen Smith* with Robert Lindsay. Peter has appeared in numerous films, such as *The Time Bandits*, *Zulu Dawn* and *The Remains of the Day*, and television shows, including the twenty-episode series *Chancer* and *Game of Thrones*. Raised in Staffordshire, Peter was educated in Uttoxeter, joining Wolverhampton Repertory Company on leaving school. During the Second World War he served in the army in France, Belgium and the Far East. His first wife was the famous actress Billie Whitelaw. He lives in West Sussex with his second wife, Lillias Walker.

**Peter Jones, 1920–2000:** Actor Peter Jones's credits are numerous. Born Peter Geoffrey F. Carey-Jones in Wem on 12 June 1920, and educated at Wem Grammar School and Ellesmere College, Peter made his stage debut at Wolverhampton's Grand Theatre. He originally made his name on radio in the 1950s, in shows such as *All Directions* with Peter Ustinov. He was also the original voice of the Guide in the radio series *The Hitchiker's Guide to the Galaxy*, before becoming equally popular on television, most famously as Mr Fenner in the popular comedy series *The Rag Trade*. Peter also appeared in *The Goodies*, *Rumpole of the Bailey*, *Holby City*, *The Bill*, *Midsomer Murders* and *Minder*, among many others, also appearing in many British films. He died in Westminster on 10 April 2000.

**Timothy Christopher:** Born just across the Welsh border in Bala on 14 October 1940, Timothy was educated at Priory Grammar School in Shrewsbury. He worked for a time at Frank Newton's Gentleman's Outfitters in Shrewsbury (where M&S is today). He is best known for his roles in the TV series *All Creatures Great and Small* and *Doctors*.

## TELEVISION

**Suzi Perry:** Born in the RAF Hospital at Cosford on 3 May 1970, television presenter Suzi was raised in Finchfield, Wolverhampton, where she attended Smethstow School, working at Wolverhampton's Grand Theatre as a lighting technician at the same time. After leaving school, Suzi studied business and finance at Wolverhampton Polytechnic, now University. Before breaking into television she worked as a model in Japan and the UK. In 2013 she was the face of Formula One on the BBC and has fronted BBC's *MotoGP* and *The Gadget Show* for Channel 5.

**Greg Davies:** The giant stand-up comedian was born 14 May 1968 in St Asaph, but grew up in Wem.

## WRITERS

**Mary Cholmondeley, 1859–1925:** Novelist Mary Cholmondeley was born in Hodnet on 8 June 1859. Together with her rector father and sister, she lived for a time at Condover Hall, which her father had inherited and where her uncle, Reginald Cholmondeley,

played host to Mark Twain on his visits to England. Mary's poetry and stories were popular towards the latter part of the nineteenth century. Known as a gentle and gracious lady, amongst her most popular works are *The Danvers Jewels* (1886), *Sir Charles Danvers* (1889) and *Red Pottage* (1899), which was a best-seller both at home and in the USA. Much of her work was published in Temple Bar. She never married, and died in Kensington on 15 July 1925.

**Mary Webb, 1881–1927:** Arguably Shropshire's most famous daughter, romantic novelist Mary Webb was passionate about the Shropshire Hills and countryside, featuring it in all of her six novels. Born Mary Meredith on 25 March 1881 in Leighton, she grew up in Much Wenlock. After marrying Henry Webb in 1912, Mary and her husband lived for a time in Pontesbury, then in Bayston Hill, near Shrewsbury. In the course of her young life she wrote many poems and short stories, plus a number of nature essays about Shropshire and its countryside. Her most famous novels are *Gone to Earth* (1917) and *Precious Bane* (1924). Mary Webb achieved most of her popular success after her death, in the 1930s. Her work has been dramatised for the theatre, film and radio. *Gone to Earth* was made into a Hollywood movie in 1950, which was filmed in Shropshire.

*Precious Bane* has been produced for TV on two separate occasions. Anyone wanting to see the places Mary wrote about should follow the Mary Webb Trails, which meander through some of the most scenic of Shropshire's landscapes. At the relatively young age of 46, Mary Webb passed away on 8 October 1927 at St Leonards on Sea, and was subsequently buried in Shrewsbury.

# 15

# SHROPSHIRE VICTORIA CROSSES

There have been four Shropshire-born winners of the Victoria Cross, whilst five others have won Britain's highest medal for bravery while serving in Shropshire regiments. Also, two former pupils of Shrewsbury School have won this highest honour for bravery.

In 1881, as part of the Childers Reforms, the 53rd Regiment was amalgamated with the 85th (Bucks Volunteers) Duke of York's Light Infantry to form the King's Shropshire Light Infantry (KSLI). Other Shropshire Units included the Shropshire Rifle Volunteers and the 86th (Shropshire) Regiment, which was raised in 1793 as a volunteer corps. The following year it was taken into the British Army, absorbing the remnants of the disbanded 118th in 1795. In 1806 the 86th became the 86th (Leinster) Regiment of foot, then six years later was renamed the 86th (Royal County Down) Regiment of Foot. The Shropshire Yeomanry, raised in 1795 as first a cavalry unit then a dismounted infantry regiment, subsequently amalgamated with the Shropshire Royal Horse Artillery, which was originally a Territorial Force formed in 1908 from the 1st Shropshire and Staffordshire Artillery Volunteers.

**Sergeant Denis Dynan, VC, 1822–63:** Born in Ireland in 1822 and described on discharge as 5ft 6.5in tall, with grey eyes, brown hair and a 'fair' complexion, labourer Denis Dynan enlisted in the 44th Regiment on 8 September 1841, transferring to the 53rd on 1 July 1844. He saw service in both the Sikh Wars, and the 1845–46 Sutlej Campaign, plus the Punjab Campaign of 1848–49.

When the Great Rebellion broke out in May 1857, the 53rd was stationed at Fort William, Calcutta. The mutineers included regiments of Bengal Infantry, part of the 8th Native Infantry, and the Ramghur Battalion. The terrified European residents fled to Hazaribagh, where the commissioner, Captain Dalton, aided by the loyal Raja of Ramghur, managed to retain order. Captain Dalton called for reinforcements and in September troops of the 53rd Regiment were diverted to Hazaribagh. The mutineers were camped 35 miles away, near the village of Chattra (also known as Chuttra or Chota Bihar). Major English led a force of the 180 men of the 53rd Regiment, plus around 150 Sikhs of the 11th Bengal Infantry and two field guns to face around 3,000 rebels. Arriving at Chattra early on 2 October 1857, Major English decided to attack without delay, putting the mutineers to flight following fierce hand-to-hand fighting in the village, losing forty-two men killed or wounded, capturing boxes of treasure, plus forty cartloads of ammunition, ten elephants and twenty teams of gun bullocks. During the fighting, two enemy guns were destroyed by artillery fire, their gun crews blown to pieces. A direct infantry attack was made on the surviving two guns, led by Lieutenant Daunt of the 11th Bengal Infantry, and Corporal Dynan of the 53rd. The first gun was taken, but the second, firing grapeshot at close range, was inflicting serious casualties, killing or wounding a third of the lieutenants' company. Daunt and Dynan rushed the gun, shooting the gun crew dead. The 53rd then marched to join Sir Colin Campbell's forces, who were trying to effect the Relief of Lucknow, playing a major role in that action and the subsequent recapture of the city.

Promoted to the rank of sergeant in July 1858, Denis Dynan served in the 53rd until his discharge in February 1861, following the regiment's return to England. Suffering from pulmonary and hepatic disease, he was admitted to the Royal Military Hospital in Kimainham, Dublin, being discharged on 1 June 1862.

It is believed that Dynan died on 16 February 1863 in Dublin, but sadly there is no record of his grave. Dynan's Victoria Cross was sold by Sothebys on 7 July 1998 for £20,000, and is now housed in the Ashcroft VC collection.

Four men of the 53rd were awarded the VC in the attack on Sikander Bagh on 16 November 1857:

**Lieutenant Alfred Kirke Ffrench, VC, 1835–72:** Ffrench was born 25 February 1835 in Meerut, India. His father was a lieutenant colonel in the 53rd Regiment, so it was only natural that young Ffrench would follow in his father's footsteps, first as ensign, then lieutenant. During the action at Lucknow, a company of the 53rd – with a troop of Bengal Horse Artillery and cavalry – formed the advance guard of the assault on Sikander Bagh, crossing a dry canal and on along a narrow lane, bordered by thickly wooded enclosures. They then turned on to a road running parallel to the Sikander Bagh, where they came under intense fire from men occupying huts and enclosures, and from the Sikander Bagh itself. This put the British soldiers in a desperate situation, their flank exposed to the enemy. In skirmish order, a company of the 53rd, took cover in the enclosures bordering the road and an artillery troop managed to climb up the steep bank, unlimbering and opening fire. A heavy battery followed and two 18-pounders punctured a hole in the wall. The assault was ordered, and included the 53rd Regiment, the 93rd Highlanders and the 4th Punjab Infantry, supported by a battalion of detachments. The 53rd lost seventy-six men killed or wounded in the action; the 93rd lost two officers and twenty men killed, and seven officers and sixty-one men wounded; the 4th Punjab lost two of four officers killed and one wounded, and sixty-nine men killed or wounded in this day's fighting and over the next few days.

Ffrench's citation reads: 'For conspicuous bravery on 16th November 1857 at the taking of the Secundra Bagh, Lucknow, when in command of the Grenadier Company, being one of the first to enter the buildings. His conduct was highly praised by the whole company.' Like many awards for bravery, Lt Ffrench was nominated by the terms of Clause 13 of the VC Warrant, via a ballot of the officers and men of his regiment.

Ffrench was advanced to captain on 3 September 1863. His VC is housed in the regimental collection in Shrewsbury Castle. Captain Ffrench died at Chiswick on 28 December 1872, and is buried in a family plot in Brompton Cemetery.

**Private James Kenny, VC, 1824–62:** Believed to have been born in Dublin, James Kenny was one of the brave soldiers of the 53rd Regiment in the attack on the Sikander Bagh in Lucknow on 16 November 1857. He was one of those chosen by ballot to receive the Victoria Cross for gallantry in the action. James's citation reads: 'For conspicuous bravery on 16th November 1857 at the taking of the Secundra Bagh, Lucknow, and for volunteering to bring up ammunition to his company under a very severe cross-fire.'

When the 53rd returned to England in 1861, Kenny chose to stay in India, transferring first to the 6th Bengal European Fusiliers, then to the 101st Regiment (later Royal Munster Fusiliers). He died of disease at Multan in the Punjab on 2–3 October 1862, and was buried in the European cemetery there.

**Private Charles Irwin, VC, 1824–73:** Born in Manorhamilton, Leitrim, Ireland, Charles enlisted in the 18th (Royal Irish) at Sligo on 4 September 1842, seeing service during the Burma Campaign in 1852–53, subsequently transferring to the 53rd Regiment. During the action at Sikander Bagh on 16 November 1857, Private Irwin, though badly wounded in the right shoulder, and under heavy fire, was one of the first to enter the building, for which he was awarded the Victoria Cross, chosen by a ballot of his comrades as per Rule 13 of the VC Warrant. His citation reads: 'For conspicuous bravery on 16th November 1857 at the taking of Secundra Bagh, Lucknow. Although severely wounded in the right shoulder, he was one of the first men of the 53rd who entered the buildings, under a very severe fire.'

Like many others of the 53rd, Charles Irwin stayed on in India, volunteering for the 87th Regiment (Royal Irish Fusiliers), which was bound for service in Hong Kong. At the time of his discharge he was described as being 40 years old, 5ft 11⅞in, with brown hair, brown eyes and a fresh complexion. He bore 'the mark of a bullet wound on his right shoulder and sabre cut to his left hand'. He died on 8 April 1873, aged 49, in Newton Butler, Fermanagh, and is buried in St Mark's churchyard, Magheraveely, Co. Fermanagh. Charles Irwin's Victoria Cross is housed in the regimental collection of the Kings Shropshire Light Infantry, in Shrewsbury Castle, along with his other campaign medals.

**Sergeant-Major Charles Pye, VC, 1820–76:** Born on 24 September 1820 at Rickerscote, Staffordshire. He enlisted in the 40th Regiment in Coventry on 18 November 1840, and served with that regiment in India before transferring to the 21st Foot, and from there to the 53rd Regiment. Another of the brave men of the 53rd to storm the Sikander Bagh on 16 November 1857, Charles Pye's case also has a specific reference to the fighting at the Mess House in Lucknow during the following day (the 17th). The strongly fortified Mess House was situated near the Sikander Bagh. Pye's citation reads: 'For steadiness and fearless conduct under fire at Lucknow on the 17th November 1857, when bringing up ammunition to the Mess House and on every occasion when the regiment has been engaged.'

Pye's Victoria Cross was another awarded under Rule 13 of the VC Warrant. The action to take the Mess House, described as a building 'of considerable size, surrounded by a loop-holed mud wall, covering a ditch about 12ft broad, scarped with masonry, the ditch traversed by drawbridges', involved a company of the 90th Foot, commanded by Captain Wolseley, together with Captain Hopkins's sixty men of the 53rd Regiment. Exposed to intense fire from neighbouring buildings, Captain Hopkins led his men at a fast pace, reaching the mud wall, then dashing across a drawbridge, and entering the Mess House.

Sergeant-Major Pye was subsequently promoted to ensign on 2 July 1858, then advanced to lieutenant when the regiment returned to England 1861, serving as adjutant in 1861–62. Upon leaving the army in 1862, Pye and his wife emigrated to New Zealand, where he became involved in the Maori Wars of 1860 to 1866, and was commissioned captain in the Colonial Defence Force (New Zealand Militia). Charles Pye died aged 56 on 14 July 1876 in Australia, whilst visiting relatives in Victoria, and was buried in the Tower Hill Cemetery at near Warrnambool.

**Private Harold Edward Whitfield, VC, 1886–1956:** Born in June 1886 in Oswestry, he enlisted in the Shropshire Yeomanry in 1908. The outbreak of the First World War in August 1914 saw the Yeomanry mobilised, and four days later they left Shropshire, expecting to be sent overseas, but instead spent the next two years as part of the English East Coast Defence Forces. The Shropshire Yeomanry finally sailed for Egypt on 3 March 1916, later joining up with other forces in May 1918 to form the 74th Yeomanry ('Broken Spur') Division. On 7 March, in the Battle of Tel Asur, the 10th Kings Shropshire Light Infantry succeeded in taking Turkish positions at Selwad. Three days later, they were ordered to seize the hill of Birj-el-Lisaneh to their north. His citation tells the story:

'For most conspicuous bravery, initiative and absolute disregard of personal safety. During the first and heaviest of three counter attacks made by the enemy on the position which had just been captured by his battalion, Pte. Whitfield, single-handed, charged and captured a Lewis gun which was harassing his company at short range. He bayoneted or shot the entire gun team and turning the gun on the enemy, drove them back with heavy casualties, thereby completely restoring the whole situation on his part of the line. Later he organised and led a bombing attack on the enemy who had established themselves in an advanced position close to our lines and from which they were enfilading his company. He drove the enemy back with great loss and by establishing his party in their position saved many lives and materially assisted in the defeat of the counter-attack.'

He was promoted to lance corporal on 7 May 1918, and then to sergeant on 10 May 1918. On 31 May 1918 Harold Whitfield received his VC from King George V at Leeds.

He was killed in a tragic road accident at the age of 70 in December 1956, hit by, of all things, a British Army vehicle whilst on his way home from work. He is buried in Oswestry. Sergeant Whitfield's VC, plus his other medals, rifle and the bayonet he actually used in winning his VC, and other personal possessions, are housed in the Shropshire Regimental Museum in Shrewsbury Castle.

During the First World War the Shropshire Yeomanry was amalgamated with the Cheshire Yeomanry, and that unit converted to infantry in Palestine in 1917, serving as the 10th (Shropshire and Cheshire Yeomanry) Battalion of the Kings Shropshire Light Infantry in 1917/18.

**Acting Sergeant George Harold Eardley, VC, MM, 1912–91:** Born on 6 May 1912 in Congleton, George enlisted in the Territorial Army on 29 March 1940, and was posted to Guildford to join the Queen's Royal Regiment (West Surreys), where first of all he was appointed acting (unpaid) lance corporal, then paid acting corporal on 23 December. He was transferred as corporal to the 4th Kings Shropshire Light Infantry on 30 July 1944, and was promoted to sergeant on 11 December 1944. George Eardley won his Military Medal in

August 1944 during fighting at the village of Le Bény-Bocage, when he stalked and destroyed a German machine-gun post.

In an odd twist, Eardley was awarded two Military Medals as a result of this action, one awarded separately and the other presented with his VC when he was invested by the king at Buckingham Palace in February 1945. One of the two MMs remains with his original medal group, now in the Ashford collection; the other was eventually sold and is now on display in the Shropshire Regimental Museum in Shrewsbury Castle.

On 13 October 1944, near St Anthonis, Sergeant Eardley was in command of a reconnaissance patrol moving towards the village of Sambeek to check on the condition of the ferry across the River Maas and the strength of nearby German defences. Next day, Eardley guided a platoon, supported by tanks, to launch a daylight raid on the German positions. Sergeant Eardley's VC citation tells the story:

'In North West Europe, on 16th [sc.15th] October 1944, during an attack on the wooded area east of Overloon, strong opposition was met from well-sited defensive positions in orchards. The enemy were paratroopers and well equipped with machine guns. A Platoon of the King's Shropshire Light Infantry was ordered to clear these orchards and restore the momentum of the advance but was halted some 80 yards from its objective by automatic fire from enemy machine gun posts. The fire was so heavy that it appeared impossible for any man to expose himself and remain unscathed. Notwithstanding this, Sergeant Eardley, who had spotted one machine gun post, moved forward, firing his Sten gun and killed the occupants of the post with a grenade. A second machine gun post beyond the first immediately opened up, spraying the area with fire. Sergeant Eardley, who was in a most exposed position, at once charged over 30 yards of open ground and silenced both the enemy gunners. The attack was continued by the Platoon but was again held up by a third machine gun post, and a section sent to dispose of it was beaten back, losing four casualties. Sergeant Eardley, ordering the section he was with to lie down, then crawled forward alone and silenced the occupants of the post with a grenade. The destruction of these three machine gun posts singlehanded by Sergt. Eardley, carried out under fire so heavy it daunted those who were with him, enabled his platoon to achieve its objective and in so doing, ensured the success of the whole attack. His outstanding initiative and magnificent bravery were the admiration of all who saw his gallant actions.'

Eardley was presented with the VC ribbon in the field by Field Marshal Montgomery. The VC medal itself was presented by the king at Buckingham Palace.

Eardley's wife was killed tragically on 25 June 1964 whilst on the way to a ceremony at Copthorne Barracks, where the Princess Royal was to present new colours to the 4th Kings Shropshire Light Infantry, when their car was hit by an express train on a level-crossing at Nantwich. George Eardley lost the lower part of his left leg, amputated on the scene of the crash without anaesthetic. He later remarried, but died only a few weeks later, on 11 September 1991, aged 79. He was cremated in Macclesfield. A replica set of George Eardley's medals, Victoria Cross, Military Medal, etc., are on show in the Shropshire Regimental Museum. A life-sized bronze statue of the war hero in battle dress, complete with Sten gun and grenade, was erected in Congleton in 2004.

**Private James Stokes, VC, 1915–45:** The 5ft 4in Scotsman James Stokes was born in Glasgow on 6 February 1915, enlisting in the Royal Artillery on 20 July 1940, spending time in the Royal Army Service Corps (52 Drivers' Training Unit), before transferring to the Gloucester Regiment in October 1943. Whilst on leave in 1944, he was sentenced to three years in prison for grievous bodily harm, or given the choice to be released into the infantry. He opted for the army, joining the Royal Warwicks, from where, in October 1944, he transferred to the 2nd Kings Shropshire Light Infantry. The battalion was then part of 185th Infantry Brigade at Overloon in Holland, with a Royal Warwicks battalion serving in the same brigade – which might explain Stokes's transfer at this time. His citation reads:

'In Holland on 1st March 1945, during the attack on Kervenheim, Pte. Stokes was a member of the leading section of a Platoon. During the advance, the Platoon came under intense rifle and medium machine gun fire from a farm building and was pinned down. The Platoon Commander began to reorganise the Platoon when Pte. Stokes, without waiting for any orders, got up and, firing from the hip, dashed through the enemy fire and was seen to disappear inside the farm building. The enemy fire stopped and Pte. Stokes reappeared with twelve prisoners. During this operation he was wounded in the neck. This action enabled the Platoon to continue the advance to the next objective and Pte. Stokes was ordered back to the Regimental Aid Post. He refused to go and continued the advance with his Platoon. On approaching the second objective, the Platoon again came under heavy fire from a house on the left. Again without waiting for orders, Pte. Stokes rushed the house by himself, firing from the hip. He was seen to drop his rifle and fall to the ground wounded. However, a moment later he got to his feet again, picked up his rifle and continued to advance, despite the most intense fire, which covered not only himself but the rest of the Platoon. He entered the house and all firing from it ceased. He subsequently rejoined his Platoon – who, due to his gallantry, had been able to advance – bringing five more prisoners. At this stage, the Company was forming up for its final assault on the objective, which was a group of buildings, forming an enemy strong point. Again without waiting for orders, Pte. Stokes, though by now severely wounded, and suffering from loss of blood, dashed down the remaining 60 yards to the objective, firing from the hip as he struggled through intense fire. He finally fell 20 yards from the enemy position, firing his rifle to the last, and as the Company passed him in the final charge, he raised his hand and shouted goodbye. Pte. Stokes was found to have been wounded eight times in the upper part of his body. Pte. Stokes's one object through out this action was to kill the enemy at whatever personal risk. His magnificent courage, devotion to duty and splendid example inspired all those round him and ensured the success of the attack at a critical moment; moreover, his self-sacrifice saved his Platoon and Company many casualties.'

Private Stokes is buried in the Reichswald Cemetery in Germany. His VC was presented to his widow and son by King George VI at Buckingham Palace. Stokes's VC and his other medals were sold by Sothebys on 21 October 1982 for £18,000 to a private collector.

**Able Seaman William Charles Williams, VC, 1880–1915:** Born at Stanton Lacy, near Ludlow, on 15 September 1880, William was raised in Chepstow. In 1895, he joined the Boys Service at Portsmouth, and was promoted to boy first-class a year later, then to able seaman in 1901. He joined the Royal Navy, but left in 1910, joining the Royal Naval Reserve whilst working as a policeman, and in a steel works. At the outbreak of the First World War he rejoined the Royal Navy.

A little after 6 a.m. on 25 April 1915, HMS *River Clyde*, an old collier, grounded its port bow on the barbed-wire strewn 'V' beach at Seddul Bahr, Cape Helles, Gallipoli, preparing to land thousands of Allied troops. Large holes had been cut in the ship's side to allow sloping gangways, suspended by wire hawsers, to be run out for the soldiers to rush down as soon as the ship grounded against the beach. Barges, made fast to the sides of the ship, formed a floating bridge in case the *River Clyde* grounded too far from the beach. Alongside were five rows of five boats each, packed with men of the Dublin Fusiliers, who were to land first to cover the disembarkation of the troops. When the soldiers of the Dublin Fusiliers leapt into the water they were immediately entangled in the wire and many were shot, as were the crews attempting to hold the boats fast. Unfortunately, the boats forming the bridge fell short of the beach, leaving a large gap that was impossible to cross, and scores of soldiers were shot by the defending Turks as they stood helpless on the uncompleted bridge. Seeing this, the ship's commander, Edward Unwin RN, and Able Seaman William Williams dropped over the side, secured a line to a drifting boat and waded through the water towing the boat towards a spit of rock that jutted from the shore. Midshipman Drewry, who was already in the water attempting to wade ashore to secure the towing rope, found that the rope they had was not long enough. Drewry returned to the ship for a longer rope while Unwin and Williams waited in chest-high water for over an hour. Williams was shot and wounded as he stood breast-deep in the water, then was killed by an exploding shell, and was carried back to the boat by Commander Unwin, who did not realise that Williams was already dead. The phenomenal bravery of the sailors from HMS *River Clyde* in maintaining the boat-bridge from the ship to the shore, and their efforts in recovering the wounded troops was recognised with six Victoria Crosses: Commander Edward Unwin (aged 51), Midshipmen George Drewry RNR (20), and Wilfred Malleson (18), Able Seaman William Williams (34), Seaman George Samson (26) and Sub-Lieutenant Arthur Tisdall (24) from the Royal Naval Division (RND).

There are two memorials to Able Seaman William Williams in Chepstow. The first is a painting of the Gallipoli action by the artist Charles Dixon, which hangs in St Mary's church. The second is a naval gun from the German submarine SM *UB-91*, which was presented by King George V, and stands proudly in the town's main square, adjacent to the town's war memorial.

**Thomas Orde Lawder Wilkinson, VC, 1894–1916:** Born at Dudmaston, near Bridgnorth in 1894, and educated at Wellington College. In 1912, the Wilkinson family emigrated to Canada, and at the outbreak of the First World War, Wilkinson enlisted in the 16th Battalion, Canadian Scottish, Canadian Expeditionary Force, later travelling to Britain, joining the 7th Battalion, Loyal North Lancashire Regiment. On the morning of the 5 July 1916, during a British attack on German trenches defending the village of La Boisselle, a separate unit was forced to retreat, abandoning its machine gun. Lieutenant Wilkinson rushed forward with two of his men, got the machine gun working and set up a rate of fire that held the advancing Germans at bay until they were relieved. Later the same day the British advance stalled under a German bombing attack, and again Wilkinson advanced, locating five soldiers who were taking cover behind a wall of earth over which the Germans were lobbing grenades. Wilkinson mounted a machine gun on top of the parapet and opened fire forcing the Germans to retreat. Brave Wilkinson was later killed while making a second attempt to bring in a wounded man from no-man's-land. He died instantly, shot through the heart, moments before he could reach the soldier. Unfortunately, it was not possible to recover his body.

Wilkinson's bravery is commemorated on the Thiepval Memorial to the Missing on the Somme, which records the names of over 72,000 men killed on the Somme and who have no known grave. His Victoria Cross is displayed at the Imperial War Museum, London.

**Captain John Henry Cound Brunt, VC, MC, 1922–44:** Born 6 December 1922 in Priest Weston, Shropshire, he joined the army as a private straight from school, and was commissioned 2 January 1943, serving with the Royal Lincolnshire Regiment, landing in Italy at Salermo on 9 September 1943. He was awarded the Military Cross and the Victoria Cross for conspicuous bravery in the face of the enemy. He died when a stray mortar shell landed at his feet and exploded.

Two Shrewsbury School ex-pupils have won the Victoria Cross:

**Thomas Tannatt Pryce, VC, MC & Bar, 1886–1918:** Pryce was born 17 January 1886 at The Hague, although his family was from Montgomeryshire. Educated at Shrewsbury School, he served originally in the Gloucester Regiment before transferring to the Grenadier Guards, where he was acting captain in the 4th Battalion. Pryce was awarded the Victoria Cross following an action at Vieux-Berquin in France on 11 April 1918, when he commanded two platoons during a successful attack on a village. Next day, Captain Pryce and his forty remaining men managed to repel four German attacks, but by evening the enemy had advanced to within 60yds of the British trench. Captain Pryce led a bayonet charge, suffering heavy casualties to drive the Germans back some 100yds. Now with only seventeen men left, and no ammunition, when the Germans attacked again, Pryce led another bayonet charge against overwhelming odds. He was last seen in the midst of fierce hand-to-hand fighting. His Victoria Cross is displayed at Regimental Headquarters of the Guards (Grenadier Guards RHQ) in London. Thomas Pryce's name is recorded on the Ploegsteert Memorial to the Missing.

**Harold Ackroyd, VC, MC, 1877–1917:** Born 18 July 1877 in Southport, Ackroyd was educated at Shrewsbury School, where he was a member of the Officers Training Corps. He went to Cambridge University, and then to Guy's Hospital in London, and from there to other hospitals, finally returning to Cambridge to become a research scholar at Downing College. Despite being involved in scientific research at Cambridge, Dr Harold Ackroyd joined up early in 1915. Commissioned temporary lieutenant in the Royal Army Medical Corps on 15 February 1915, and attached to the 6th Battalion of the Royal Berkshire Regiment (which in turn formed part of the 53rd Infantry Brigade in the 18th Division), he was sent to the front on the Somme. By the end of 1915, the 18th Division had suffered 1,247 casualties. The Battle of Passchendaele began on 31 July 1917, and the 18th Division became involved in a huge military blunder. The infantry of the 30th Division assaulted Chateau Wood, which was occupied by the British, instead of the German positions in Glencorse Wood, their intended target. Ackroyd's 53rd Brigade plunged into the intended target unsupported, with fatal consequences. For the rest of that day, and the next, the 53rd Brigade attempted to dislodge a well-defended German position. A fellow officer recorded that 'in all that hellish turmoil, there was one quiet figure, most heroic, most wonderful of all, Dr Ackroyd, the 6th Berks Medical Officer, a stooping, grey haired, bespectacled man who rose to the supreme heights that day, seeming to be everywhere, tending to, and bandaging scores of men.' Passchendaele resulted in twenty-three separate VC recommendations for Captain Ackroyd. Harold Ackroyd died on 11 August 1917 in Jargon Trench on the western edge of Glencorse Wood when he was shot in the head by a sniper. His body was allegedly evacuated and buried in Birr Cross Roads Cemetery near Ypres and his headstone reads: 'Believed to be buried in this cemetery'. His citation reads:

'For most conspicuous bravery. During recent operations Capt. Ackroyd displayed the greatest gallantry and devotion to duty. Utterly regardless of danger, he worked continuously for many hours up and down and in front of the line tending the wounded and saving the lives of officers and men. In so doing he had to move across the open under heavy machine-gun, rifle and shell fire. He carried a wounded officer to a place of safety under very heavy fire. On another occasion he went some way in front of our advanced line and brought in a wounded man under continuous sniping and machine-gun fire. His heroism was the means of saving many lives, and provided a magnificent example of courage, cheerfulness, and determination to the fighting men in whose midst he was carrying out his splendid work. This gallant officer has since been killed in action.'

Two other VCs are mentioned in the KSLI Regimental Museum in Shrewsbury Castle: Captain Godfrey Meynell, VC, MC, of the 2nd–12th Frontier Force Regiment, Indian Army Corps of Guides, ex 1 KSLI, was awarded the VC for action on 29 September 1935. Acting Assistant Commissar James Langby Dalton, VC, ex 85th/53rd Regiment, received the VC for the action at Rorke's Drift, 22–23 January 1879.

All courageous men who will never be forgotten.

# 16

# MISCELLANEOUS

## LITERATURE, TELEVISION AND FILM

Famous American writer Mark Twain used to stay at Condover Hall on his visits to England.

In the summer of 2004, film star Harrison Ford, his actress wife, Calista Flockhart, and their two kids, spent a holiday on the Llangollen Canal in Shropshire.

In 2006 the film *Atonement* – starring Keira Knightly and James McAvoy, and based upon Ian McEwan's novel of the same name – was partly filmed around Stokesay Court.

Shropshire is regularly chosen by filmmakers as a backdrop for box office hits that are seen all over the world. Perhaps the all-time classic is the evocative adaptation of Mary Webb's novel *Gone to Earth*, which was filmed around Much Wenlock and the Stiperstones in 1949.

Richard Burton also popped by to film *Absolution* in 1978, which was filmed at Ellesmere College, although regrettably both critics and public alike considered it 'not one of Burton's best films'!

A lot of films have been shot in and around Much Wenlock, such as the 1980 comedy film *Clockwise* starring John Cleese.

In 1984, the cast and crew of an adaptation of Charles Dickens's *A Christmas Carol*, starring the American actor George C. Scott, transformed Shrewsbury from modern-day county town into snowy Victorian England. The production team took over the whole of the Prince Rupert Hotel. The graveyard of St Chad's church has an odd claim to fame for it houses (if that's the correct word) the grave of Ebenezer Scrooge. However, this is a big hoax! The grave was created for a scene in the film, but when filming was completed the crew left the grave at the location. Much of the film was shot in Fish Street.

Hugh Grant's film, *The Englishman Who Went Up a Hill but Came Down a Mountain* was filmed at Hampton Loade and other locations near to Oswestry.

The Oscar-winning drama *Howards End* brought big names like Anthony Hopkins and Emma Thompson to Brampton Bryan, just across the border from Ludlow.

It's not just on the big screen that Shropshire has been seen. Television crews have also filmed all over the county, producing *Oliver Twist*, *The Pickwick Papers* and *Oh, Doctor Beeching*, among many others.

Some of our top attractions, such as Hawkstone Park and Follies and the Ironbridge Gorge Museums, have also been seen on the small screen. Hawkstone was the perfect setting for the BBC adaptation of *The Chronicles of Narnia*, and Ludlow Castle was the centrepiece for ITV's *Moll Flanders*.

This celebrity fascination with our area shows no signs of slowing. In 2005, Chirk Castle was chosen as one of the locations for the BBC's version of *Casanova*. You may also have spotted John Challis (Boysie of *Only Fools and Horses* fame) filming the spin-off *The Green, Green Grass* in the countryside around Ludlow.

And if you were around Blists Hill in 1985, you'd have seen Kate O'Mara in leather trousers doing battle with Colin Baker as Doctor Who.

Tom Sharpe's *Blott on the Landscape* was filmed in Ludlow.

# OTHER

Here's an unusual connection with Shropshire: legendary reggae singer Bob Marley's father, Norval Marley, enlisted in the army in 1916 in Liverpool. He was sent for training to Park Hall Camp, Oswestry, but Norval was not a strong man and was deemed not fit enough to fight. He spent the war in England, serving with a Works Battalion whose jobs included preparing food, laundry and sewerage. He later travelled to Jamaica, where he met and married 18-year-old Cedella Malcolm; Norval was 60, and in February 1945 Nesta Robert Marley (Bob) was born. The couple separated not long after. Norval died when Bob was 10.

Until the Counties (Detached Parts) Act 1844, the townships of Halesowen, Cakemore, Hasbury, Hawne, Illey, Lapal, Ridgeacre, Hunnington, Oldbury and Romsley (all in the parish of Halesowen) were detached parts of the county of Shropshire. On 20 October 1844 they were transferred to Worcestershire. The chapelry of Farlow in the parish of Stottesdon was transferred to Herefordshire.

The 1987 Suntory World Matchplay final was contested by two Shropshire-born golfers: Sandy Lyle and Ian Woosnam. Woosie won, setting a new record of 32 under par for his 4 rounds. Both went on to win the US Masters at Augusta National Golf Club: Lyle in 1988, Woosie in 1991.

Woolstaston was originally known as Wulverstanton due the preponderance of wolves that previously roamed thereabouts.

Prime Minister Benjamin Disraeli was Tory MP for Shrewsbury 1841–47.

In 1998 Western Park hosted the G8 Summit.

In November 1883, turnpike road gates were removed in Shropshire.

Shropshire is the home of the British Hedgehog Society, a charity started by Major Adrian Coles. The society concerns itself with improving the welfare of wildlife, and with such innovations as providing hedgehog ramps in cattle grids, which prevent the little spiky creatures from getting trapped and injured.

Tory MP for Bridgnorth (1771–95), Thomas Whitmore (1743–95) drowned in a well in his garden.

Henry Eckford of Wem is the man responsible for developing one of the most popular flowering plants – the sweet pea. He created the highly scented plant after many years of crossbreeding. Wem holds a sweet pea festival every year in July.

Just outside Wellington, sheep steeplechasing takes place at Hoo Farm; the sheep wear woolly jockeys on their backs. Visitors are invited to place bets on which sheep will cross the winning line first.

The very delicious but extremely smelly Shropshire Blue Cheese is not actually made in Shropshire. Most of it is made in Leicestershire and Nottinghamshire. Whitchurch, Shropshire, is the home of Cheshire Cheese.

The Aga cooker, that ultimate symbol of homeliness (which is manufactured in Shropshire) has become a worldwide favourite with the great and the good. Ask renowned cookery writer and TV expert Mary Berry, and you'll immediately know why.

In the fifteenth and sixteenth centuries, the churchyard of St Alkmund's in Shrewsbury was used as a cattle market.

In 1836–38 the timings for the stagecoach journey from London to Holyhead on the New Holyhead Mail coach were as follows: depart London at 8 p.m., arrive Shifnal (137½ miles) at 10.14 a.m., arrive Haygate (141½ miles) at 10.59 a.m., arrive Shrewsbury (152 miles) at 11.59 a.m. and depart at 12.04 p.m., arrive Nesscliffe (160½ miles) at 12.53 p.m., arrive Oswestry (170 miles) at 1.46 p.m., arrive Llangollen (182½ miles) at 2.58 p.m., arrive Holyhead (260½ miles) at 19.55 p.m. The fare for the full route was £3 inside the coach and £1 10*s* outside. The fare to Shrewsbury was £1 inside and 10*s* outside.

Another Tory MP for Bridgnorth (1818–20), Sir Thomas Tyrwhitt-Jones, 2nd Baronet (1793–1839) was accidentally shot on a hunt.

John Wesley preached his first sermon in Shrewsbury on 16 March 1761 at No. 1 Fish Street. He made at least seventeen visits to the town.

During the Napoleonic Wars, before inheriting Aldenham Hall, Sir John Acton was prime minister to King Ferdinand IV of Naples.

Yet another MP for Bridgnorth was Roundhead Edmund Waring (1620–82) (High Sheriff of Shrewsbury 1657–59, Governor of Shrewsbury 1659–60), who apparently drowned in a pond after drinking and carousing to celebrate the execution of King Charles I.

In pagan times metallic objects were thrown into wells, often known later as pin wells, to placate the gods for robbing them of their metal (ore). John Wesley is reputed to have drunk from the pin well in Dawley.

# 17

# MILITARY CONNECTIONS

## SHIPS

Unusually for a landlocked county, a number of ships have been named after parts of the county:

HMS *Shropshire* was a Royal Navy heavy cruiser of the London sub-class of County-class cruisers. This was the only warship to hold this name and was laid down at the William Beardmore and Company shipyard in Dalmuir, Scotland and launched by Violet Herbert, Countess of Powis on 5 July 1928. Fitted out for sea on 12 September 1929, she served until 1942, when she was transferred to the Royal Australian Navy, following her sister ship, HMS *Canberra*. Commissioned HMAS *Shropshire*, the ship remained in service until 1949, when she was sold for scrap in 1954. She took part in the last great surface engagement at the Battle of Surigao Strait, and was present at the Japanese surrender at Tokyo Bay in September 1945.

Three ships have born the name of the county town, and one had that of the castle. The first HMS *Shrewsbury* was an eighty-gun, three-decker ship-of-the-line launched at Portsmouth dockyard 6 February 1695. Part of Vice-Admiral Edward Vernon's fleet, which took part in the expedition to Cartagena de Indias during the War of Jenkin's Ear. She narrowly escaped destruction on the infamous Goodwin Sands during the great storm of 26 November 1703. Rebuilt in 1706, she was relaunched in 1713, and broken up in 1749. The second was a seventy-four-gun third-rate launched at Deptford in 1758, condemned in 1783 and scuttled off Jamaica that same year. The third was a Hunt-class minesweeper launched in 1918 and sold in 1927. HMS *Shrewsbury Castle* was a Castle-class corvette launched in 1943. She was loaned to the Royal Norwegian Navy in 1944 and renamed HNoMS *Tunsberg Castle*, and sunk by a mine that same year.

Three ships have proudly carried the name of *Ludlow*. The first was a thirty-two-gun fifth-rate frigate, launched in 1698. The second a First World War auxiliary paddle-minesweeper. She was laid down 1 May 1916 and sunk by a mine 29 December 1916. The third, a destroyer originally named USS *Stockton*, an American Caldwell-class destroyer, was laid down at the shipyard of William Cramp and Sons, Philadelphia, Pennsylvania. Out of commission until 1940, she was shuttled to Halifax, Nova Scotia, where she was decommissioned and handed over to the UK. She served in the Royal Navy as HMS *Ludlow*, rated a Town-class destroyer, until decommissioned in June 1945. Beached off Fidra Island, Firth of Forth, and used as a rocket target by the RAF, she sank in 6m of water off Yellowcraigs beach.

Two ships have borne the name HMS *Ludlow Castle*. Both fifth-rate frigates, the first was launched in 1707 and broken up in 1721; the second was launched in 1724 and broken up in 1749.

Nine ships have been named after the River Severn. The first was a fifty-gun, fourth-rate, two-decked ship-of-the-line launched at Blackwall Yard in 1695 was broken up and rebuilt as the second HMS *Severn* in 1739, serving until 1746 when she was captured by the French Navy. Recaptured by the Royal Navy off Cape Finisterre on 14 June 1747, she was relaunched as the third warship to bear this name. She was sold in 1759. The fourth ship of this name was a forty-four-gun Adventure-class fifth-rate launched in 1786 and wrecked in 1804. The fifth was a forty-gun Endymion-class fourth-rate ship built in fir softwood, which proved leaky and unseaworthy. She served off Algiers in 1816 and was broken up in 1825. The sixth was one of the last sailing warship frigates, built in 1856 and broken up in 1876. The seventh HMS *Severn* was a Mersey-class protected cruiser, a solely steam-powered vessel with no sailing rig, built in 1885. The eighth HMS *Severn* was an

Amazon river monitor. A specialist shore bombardment vessel built by Vickers for Brazil in 1914, she saw service at Konigsberg in 1915 and was sold for scrap in 1921. The ninth HMS *Severn* was a Thames-class fleet submarine built in 1934. She served in the South Atlantic following the outbreak of the Second World War, Norway in 1940, the Atlantic in 1940–41, Sicily and the Aegean in 1943. She was scrapped in 1946.

Ditton Priors Royal Navy Armament Depot was built in 1941 and used by the navy until 1965, when it was taken over by US Forces after they left France. The depot housed twenty-five magazines and four mine stores, and finally closed in 1968. It is now used as an industrial estate and a fireworks factory.

Shropshire has connections with other branches of the services, with RAF stations at Shawbury and Cosford, and many more during wartime. Lists of these can be found on the Shropshire History website. The army depot at Donnington was once one of the largest in the UK.

# 18

# WATER AND WATERWAYS

## RIVERS

Shropshire has many watercourses running through its lands; the two main rivers are the Severn and the Teme.

**River Severn:** Britain's longest river at 220 miles (354km) (only the River Shannon in Ireland is longer in the British Isles). The source of the Severn is at Plynlimon in the Cambrian Mountain range in Ceredigian, Wales, at an altitude of 2,001ft (610m), flowing through Ceredigian, Powys, Shropshire, Worcestershire and Gloucestershire on its route to the Bristol Channel. Into the Shropshire Severn run the rivers Perry, Rea, Tern, Cound and the Worfe. In Wales its main tributary is the Vyrnwy, and further downstream the Teme, the Warwickshire Avon and the Stour. The River Wye runs into the Severn Estuary at Chepstow. The Severn has twenty-one tributaries in total.

The Severn Bore is a tidal surge caused when the rising tidal water is funnelled up the Severn Estuary against the flow of the river. This often spectacular phenomenon can be witnessed on a number of occasions during the year, but it is usually largest in spring. The Severn Bore can reach speeds of up to 13mph and the highest recorded wave was 9.2ft, on 15 October 1966. The longest surfboard ride was 5.7 miles.

The River Severn's Welsh name is Afon Hafren; its Latin (Roman) name was Sabrina after a mythical water nymph.

**River Teme:** Like the Severn, the source of the Teme is in Wales, beginning its journey at an altitude of 1,660ft (506m) on Cilfaesty Hill in the Kerry Hills, south of Newtown in Powys, joining the Severn at

Powick, south of Worcester. Into the Teme run the rivers Clun, Onny, Corve and another Rea. At 60 miles (96km) long, the Teme is the sixteenth-longest river in the UK. Its Welsh name is Afon Tefeidiad.

# CANALS

The 67-mile (108km) **Shropshire Union Canal** is the county's longest man-made watercourse, and links the West Midlands to the River Mersey at Ellesmere Port. It joins the Staffordshire and Worcester Canal at Autherley Junction, Oxley Moor, Wolverhampton.

The **Llangollen Canal** passes through Shropshire more or less east–west, joining the Shropshire Union Canal at Hurleston Junction, near Nantwich, and running to Llangollen in Wales.

The 35-mile (56km) **Montgomery Canal** joins the Llangollen Canal at Lower Frankton in Shropshire, and runs down to Newtown in Wales. Eleven miles (18km) of its length runs through Shropshire.

There are/were a number of other canals in the county:

The 5.5 mile, seven-lock **Donnington Wood Canal**, also known as the Marquess of Stafford's Canal and the Duke of Sutherland's Canal, it was completed in 1767, joining with the Wombridge Canal in 1788.

The **Ketley Canal**, 1.5 miles long with one lock, opened in 1788, joined to the Shropshire Canal in 1791, and was closed in 1880.

The **Shrewsbury and Newport Canal**, 2.75 miles long with nine locks, opened in 1794. In 1796, a further 14.5-mile section with two locks was opened from Wappenshall Junction to Shrewsbury Basin (including the Berwick Tunnel). A 105-mile section with twenty-three locks was added in 1835, linking Wappenshall Junction with Norbury Junction and joined to the Wombridge Canal.

The 7.75-mile **Shropshire Canal** opened in 1790, from Donnington Wood to the River Severn at Coalport. The 2.75-mile Coalbrookdale Branch was opened in 1792, connecting the Hay Incline Plane to Southall Bank.

The 1.75-mile **Wombridge Canal** opened in 1788, running from Old Yard Junction at Dinnington Wood to Wombridge Tunnel, linking with the Ketley and the Shropshire Union canals.

Three other Shropshire canals were the **Birmingham and Liverpool Junction Canal**, the **Eardington Canal** and the **Leominster Canal**. There were also several underground canals in the Telford area, the most famous being the Tar Tunnel at Coalport.

## MERES AND LAKES

Eighteen thousand years ago, mountain-high sheets of ice stretched across north Shropshire. It melted very slowly over 1,000 years as the Ice Age thawed, leaving behind Shropshire's wonderfully distinctive landscape of hills and valleys dotted with dozens of lakes and meres. All dimensions are approximate due to natural movement.

Around Ellesmere is an area that many have called Shropshire's Lake District, with a host of glacial meres, including The Mere, Blake Mere, Kettle Mere, White Mere, Newton Mere, Cole Mere, Crose Mere and Sweat Mere.

The Mere, near Ellesmere, is the largest of the meres with a surface area of 107.2 acres (43.4 ha). It is 1.5km long, 0.5km wide and 19m deep, with a perimeter of 1.9 miles (3km), and is packed with fish and wildlife.

Blake Mere is 416m long, covering an area of around 7.9 acres (3.2 ha), around 12ft deep and with a perimeter of 0.6 miles (0.9km). It was once called Black Mere because of its peaty-coloured water.

Kettle Mere, almost attached to Blake Mere, is one of the smallest of the meres around Ellesmere.

White Mere is 630m long, has a surface area of 58.1 acres (23.5 ha) and a 1.2-mile (1.9km) perimeter.

Newton Mere has a surface area of 20.3 acres (8.2 ha), is 403m long, with a perimeter of 0.7 miles (1.2km).

Cole Mere, a classic kettle hole mere, is 868m long, with a surface area of 67 acres (27.1 ha) and perimeter of 1.6 miles (2.6km).

Crose Mere covers an area of around 37.6 acres (15.2 ha). It is 792m long and 300m wide, and at least 9m deep, with a perimeter of 1.1 miles (1.8km).

Sweat Mere was once joined to Crose Mere when the water level in the area was considerably higher. It is 75m long of open water, with a dimension of around 140–150m in total, including reedswamp, and around 2m deep with a surface area of 2.2 acres (0.9 ha).

Other substantial bodies of water in the country are:

Aqualate Mere, near Newport (technically just across the border in Staffordshire). This is the largest lake in the Midlands at 1.5km long and 0.5km wide, but is shallow at around 1m deep. Its unusual name derives from the Anglo-Saxon 'Ac-gelad', meaning Oak Grove.

Ossmere near Whitchurch is 551m long, with a surface area of 25.9 acres (10.5 ha), and a perimeter of 0.9 miles (1.4km).

Bomere Pool, near Condover, though not part of the Shropshire Lake District, is worth a mention. Covering an area of around 25 acres (10.3 ha), the pool is around 50ft (15.2m) deep. This privately owned mere has been classed a 'Site of Special Interest' because it is the most nutrient-poor body of water in the county. Not far from Bomere Pool, on a September evening in 1986, Eve Roberts made a fantastic discovery while out walking her dogs. She saw large bones sticking up out of the clay in a gravel quarry. They turned out to be those of a female woolly mammoth, and three young mammoths, one about 6 years old, and two around 4 years old. A full-sized replica of the adult mammoth's skeleton can be seen at the Secret Hills Exhibition.

Nearby is Betton Pool, 63m long, with a surface area of 14.6 acres (5.9 ha), and in between the two is the much smaller Shomere Pool, surface area 3.2 acres (1.3 ha), 138m long with a perimeter of 0.3 miles (0.4km).

Hawk Lake near Weston-Under-Redcastle is 887m long, surface area 38.1 acres (15.4 ha) with a perimeter of 3 miles (4.9km).

Llyn Rhuddwyn near Oswestry, has a surface area of 4.2 acres (1.7 ha), a perimeter of 0.3 miles (0.5km) and is 165m long.

Polemere near Shrewsbury is 158m long, has a surface area of 3.7 acres (1.5 ha) and a perimeter of 0.3 miles (0.5km).

Berrington Pool near Cross Houses is 206m long with a surface area of 6.2 acres (2.5 ha).

Fenemere near Baschurch has a surface area of 23.2 acres (9.4 ha), and is 458m long with a perimeter of 0.8 miles (1.2km).

Norton Mere near Tong is 899m long, its surface area is 24.5 acres (9.9 ha) and its perimeter is 1.4 miles (2.3km).

Just over the border in Cheshire are a number of other meres: Quoisley Big Mere, Quoisley Little Mere, Big Mere and Little Mere.

# WELLS

Shropshire has many historic or symbolic wells. Here are just a few of them:

- The Holy Well – near Tibberton
- The Bony Well – between Ludlow and Richard's Castle
- Boiling Wells – in Ludlow, Gorsty, and Long Mynd
- Inflammable Well – in Broseley
- The Old Well – at Great Nesscliffe
- St Oswald's Well – Oswestry
- St Milburga's Well – in Much Wenlock
- Pitch Well – near Pitchford Hall, is a bituminous spring
- Potseething Well – Oldbury
- Frog Well – Acton Burnell

# 19

# CASTLES AND FORTIFICATIONS

As one would expect with a county bordering Wales, Shropshire's stormy history has left us with a littering of more than our fair share of fortifications: thirty-two castles and twenty-five hill forts, plus two dykes – Offa's Dyke (built by King Offa in the eighth century, probably to keep the Welsh princes at bay) and Wat's Dyke.

**Acton Burnell Castle:** Construction of this red-sandstone structure is believed to have been started in 1283 by Robert Burnell (see People), Chancellor of England and a personal friend of King Edward I, as a replacement for an earlier building which was home to the Burnell family, from whom the castle and settlement take their name. The building is really a fortified manor house, built for comfort rather than defence. The nearby barn is the site of the first Parliament at which the commons were formally represented. The king granted Robert Burnell licence to crenelate the castle, but sadly none of the fortifications remain. The Burnell male line came to a halt in 1402, and from then on the castle fell into a state of disrepair, ownership passing through a number of hands. In 1672, the Smythe family decided the castle would be better as a folly. The site is now in the care of English Heritage.

**Bridgnorth Castle:** The ruins of the 70ft twelfth-century Norman keep of Bridgnorth Castle leans over at an angle of 15°, three times more than the Leaning Tower of Pisa. The keep, besides a few other pieces of stonework, is all that is left of this once imposing fortress sitting atop a narrow promontory that towers over the west bank of the River Severn. The castle was founded by Robert de Bellême, 3rd Earl of Shrewsbury, in 1101. Originally known as Brug, or Bruges, the town of Bridgnorth grew up around the castle. In 1102, Earl Robert backed the wrong side by supporting Robert Curthose, Duke of Normandy, in his attempt to depose his younger brother, King Henry I. The king successfully besieged and took the castle, turning it into a royal stronghold. Sadly for Bellême, he was stripped of his titles, the earldom disappearing for centuries, and the castle was allowed to deteriorate. However, five centuries later and still a royal fortress and garrisoned by Royalist troops, Bridgnorth Castle hosted a visit by King Charles I following his 'Wellington Declaration' in October 1642, on his way to Edge Hill for first battle of the English Civil War. Then, in 1646, the re-strengthened castle was besieged by Oliver Cromwell's Parliamentarians. Following fierce fighting, the Roundheads broke through the palisade into St Leonard's Close on 31 March, killing the Royalist leader, Colonel Billingsley. The retreating Royalists set alight houses in the High Street as a delaying tactic, and the fire spread, blowing up the ammunition store housed in St Leonard's church. The Parliamentarians laid siege to the castle, which finally capitulated on 26 April 1646. Cromwell ordered the dismantling of the castle and by early 1647 their destructive work was complete. Stone from the castle was used to repair damaged buildings in the town.

**Clun Castle:** The original Norman timber motte-and-bailey-style castle was built some time around 1100, by Robert 'Picot' de Say (de Sai), on land owned by Edric Silvaticus (Edric the Wild). In time, the wooden structure was rebuilt in stone. In 1196, the Welsh under Lord Rhys besieged the castle. Ownership subsequently passed to the Fitz Alans, who lived there until some time in the 1270s, when they moved to Arundel Castle in Sussex. The castle then began to fall into ruin. The Welsh patriot Owain Glyn Dwr attacked the castle on one of his rampages, but as the years passed Clun's importance diminished. The ruins of the 80ft Norman keep still stands proud on the

CLUN CASTLE

castle mound. In the mid-sixteenth century, ownership passed to the Howard family (Dukes of Norfolk), who sold it to the Earl of Northampton, then bought it back in the 1890s.

**Hopton Castle:** Originally a Norman timber motte-and-bailey construction, Hopton Castle was built by Walter de Hopton some time after the Norman invasion. The later stone castle was built at the time of the Second Barons' War in the 1260s and the centrepiece was an impressive rectangular two-storey keep. Ownership passed to the Corbet family of Moreton Corbet, subsequently passing through marriage to Sir Henry Wallop, a wealthy Hampshire gentleman who fortified the castle for Parliament. His son Robert was one of the 135 commissioners to judge King Charles I, but he did not actually sign the king's death warrant. Hopton Castle was the scene of one of the bloodiest episodes of the Civil War (see The Siege at Hopton Castle in Battles, Skirmishes and Sieges).

**Ludlow Castle:** Construction of Ludlow Castle began in the late eleventh century as the border stronghold of Marcher Lord Roger De Lacy. Then early in the fourteenth century it was enlarged to create a magnificent palace for Roger Mortimer, then the most powerful man in England, subsequently passing through marriage to Richard, Duke of York. During the Wars of the Roses the castle remained a Yorkist stronghold, before once again becoming a royal palace. In 1472, Yorkist King Edward IV sent his two sons, Edward, Prince of Wales and Richard of Shrewsbury, Duke of York (later known as the Princes in the Tower) to live at the castle, which at that time was also the seat of government for Wales and the border counties. In 1501, during the reign of Henry VII, his son Arthur, Prince of Wales (older brother of Henry, later Henry VIII) and his new bride Catherine of Aragon lived in the castle for a time before his untimely death. Princess Mary Tudor (later Queen Mary) and her court spent three winters at Ludlow between 1525 and 1528. In 1646, Ludlow Castle was lost to the Royalists by Prince Rupert of the Rhine, causing the king to fall out with his cousin. Fortunately, because the Royalist garrison negotiated a surrender to avoid damage and slighting, the Roundheads didn't completely destroy this magnificent castle as they had Bridgnorth. In 1689, Lord Herbert of Chirbury founded the Royal Welsh Fusiliers at the castle, but not long afterwards the fortress was abandoned and fell into decay. In 1811, the 2nd Earl of Powis purchased the ruins from the crown and the castle has remained in the family since then. The highly picturesque and imposing Ludlow Castle occupies a well-judged position standing on high ground, flanked by two rivers, the Teme and the Corve.

**Moreton Corbet Castle:** This magnificent and unusual ornate ruin is in the village of Moreton Corbet near Shawbury. Originally known as the castle at Moreton Toret, it was built by Bartholomew Torret following the Norman Conquest. Some time around 1239, the estate passed to the Corbet family, who built a stone castle on the site. What was left of the Norman keep and gatehouse were later incorporated into an Elizabethan manor house. The castle was fortified and garrisoned for the king during the Civil War by Sir Vincent Corbet, with a force of 110 men. After being tricked in the middle of the night, the Royalist defenders surrendered and the castle was taken. The Roundheads then burned it down.

**Shrewsbury Castle:** This Norman castle was originally built in 1070 by Roger de Montgomery, Earl of Shrewsbury, on the site of an earlier Anglo-Saxon fortification, to guard the open end of a loop in the River Severn, which was to all effects a massive moat. Much of the castle was demolished during the reign of King Edward I to allow a rebuilding and strengthening programme to take place, but like so many other fortifications, during the 1500s the Norman red-standstone castle was allowed to fall into disrepair. It was garrisoned for the king at the start of the Civil War, but was captured in 1645 by a Parliamentarian force. In 1660 the castle was surrendered to the crown following the restoration of King Charles II. In 1663, the king granted the castle to Sir Francis Newport of High Ercall, and in 1924 it was acquired by the Corporation of Shrewsbury, who undertook a process of restoration and opened the castle to the public in 1926. Shrewsbury Castle now houses the Shropshire Regimental Museum.

**Stokesay Castle:** Near Craven Arms, this is not strictly a castle in the truest sense, it is really more of a medieval fortified manor house, but it is probably the finest and best preserved in England, surviving the ravages of time completely intact. Having begun its life in late Norman times, Stokesay Castle dates back to some time around 1281, when it was built by Lawrence of Ludlow, a leading wool merchant. In Elizabethan times the stunning timber-framed Jacobean gatehouse was built, the ornately carved timbers over the gatehouse entrance depicting Adam and Eve in the Garden of Eden. In June 1645, it was briefly besieged by a force of Parliamentarians, who soon forced the garrison to surrender. The castle was ordered to be slighted, but fortunately little damage was done to the walls. Perhaps the Roundheads liked the way it looked. The castle was allowed to deteriorate until the 1980s, when English Heritage took over its care and carried out extensive renovations.

**Whittington Castle:** This castle was built by the Normans some time after Domesday Book because there is no mention of it in that extensive tome. In fact, the first mention of a castle at Whittington dates to 1138, when a motte-and-bailey-style timber fortification was built by William Peverel. He was reputed to be one of the Conqueror's bastards, and was a lord who supported the claims of the Empress Matilda in her long-running battle for the English Crown against King Stephen. When William Peverel's grandson, also William, died leaving no male heir, his daughter Mellette inherited the castle, and a tournament was held, with the victor to become her husband. The winner was Warine de Metz. Their son, Fulk FitzWarine, was knighted by Henry I. In 1200, Fulk FitzWarine III rebelled against King John for three years, disputing the ownership of the castle, which had been granted to Roger de Powis. For this he was declared an outlaw, which has been said to be the basis for the legend of Robin Hood. Fulk was forced to flee to France, but was eventually pardoned by King John, who in 1204 granted Whittington Castle to the FitzWarine family. Fulk FitzWarine III was one of the powerful barons who in 1215 forced King John to sign Magna Carta. Around 1221 Fulk built a stone castle which, like many others, replaced the earlier timber structure, that itself was constructed on the site of an earlier stronghold from the time of King Offa. In 1223, Llewelyn ap Iorwerth of Gwynedd and his Welsh raiders destroyed the castle and it had to be rebuilt. In 1265, Whittington Castle was granted by King Henry III to Llewelyn ap Gruffudd, with Hamo le Strange acting

WHITTINGTON CASTLE

as custodian since Fulk FitzWarine V was still a minor. In 1420 Fulk FitzWarine XIV died, ending the long line of FitzWarine owners of the castle. It was only in 1536 that Whittington became part of Shropshire, when the Act of Union abolished the Marcher Lordships. In 1545, the castle was sold to the crown and then fell into disrepair. During the English Civil War the dilapidated castle was held for the king, eventually being partially destroyed by Parliamentarian cannon fire in 1643. The ruined castle is now owned by the local community and is open to visitors.

**Caus Castle:** Built in the 1070s by William Corbet, Caus Castle guarded the road from Shrewsbury to Montgomery. Suspected to stand partly on the site of an Iron Age fort. There is a high motte with a small summit, on which now stand the ruins of a small stone tower with an inner bailey. Caus Castle takes its rather odd-sounding name from the original home of the Corbet family, Pays de Caux in Normandy. In the late twelfth century a borough was founded in the large outer bailey of the castle. During the rebellion of the Welsh Prince Owain Glyn Dwr in the 1400s, Caus was garrisoned by Gruffydd ap Ieuan ap Madoc ap Gwenwys against the Welsh raiders, but Gruffydd changed sides and supported Glyn Dwr, forfeiting the castle in 1404. In 1419, King Henry V restored the fortifications in thanks to Gruffydd's sons for capturing the outlaw John Oldcastle. But in 1443, after those same two sons and their followers were found to have murdered Sir Christopher Talbot, Champion Jouster of England and son of John Talbot, Earl of Shrewsbury, their family lands were once again forfeited, and over time the castle was allowed to fall into disrepair. During the Civil War, the castle was garrisoned for the king but was subsequently destroyed by Parliamentarian forces.

**Oswestry Castle:** Dating back to around 1086, Domesday Book records Oswestry Castle as being built by Rainald, Sheriff of Shropshire. Before that the site may have been a frontier Welsh and Anglo-Saxon outpost. William the Conqueror granted the area to Roger de Montgomery, and it subsequently passed to the Fitz Alan family. Between 1149 and 1157, Oswestry Castle was held by Madoc ap Maerdydd (Meredith), Prince of Powys, but King Henry II returned it to the Fitz Alans. Henry II also used the castle as a base for his campaigns against the Welsh. Oswestry Castle became a strategic military stronghold again when Civil War broke out in 1642, and was reinforced when the town declared for King Charles I and the Royalist cause (see Siege of Oswestry in Battles, Skirmishes and Sieges). At the end of the Civil War, Oswestry Castle was all but completely destroyed by the Parliamentarians.

**Shrawardine Castle:** One of two fortifications built on either side of a ford across the River Severn. In 1212, Prince Llewelyn and his Welsh raiders destroyed the castle. It was rebuilt by the Fitz Alans, who renamed it Castle Isabel and held it until forced to sell the estate in 1583. The Royalists held the castle at the start of the English Civil War, but after Shrewsbury was captured by the Parliamentarians in 1645, Shrawardine too was taken, slighted and subsequently fell into disrepair.

**Holdgate Castle:** Also known as Holgate Castle, Helgots Castle, or Castle Holegod, or Stanton Holegate/Long, this multi-named

Norman castle situated in a village that itself has three names: Holdgate, Stanton Holdgate and Castle Holdgate. There's not much of this fortification left to see. It was built some time before Domesday Book by a Norman named Helgot de Reisolent. When he died, his son, Herbert Fitz Helgot, inherited the castle, and in 1109 entertained King Henry I there (Castrum Helgot). Later owned for a time by the Knights Templar, the castle then fell into ruin. During the Civil War the site was refortified, then in 1644 it was besieged by the Royalists, who inflicted heavy damage. Some stone foundations remain, and the ruins of a thirteenth-century semi-circular tower were incorporated into the farmhouse that now occupies the site.

**Bishop's Castle:** The town is named after what once stood on the site – a castle built by a bishop in 1087 – the Bishop of Hereford to be more accurate. The original structure was a typical motte-and-bailey castle built to defend the church and area from marauding Welsh raiders. It was damaged in 1263 when John FitzAlan, Earl of Arundel, Lord of Oswestry and Clun besieged the castle. In the early Middle Ages the castle and parish straddled the English–Welsh border. Around the early 1600s, the king granted the castle to the

ELIZABETHAN
GATEHOUSE

Howards, who allowed it to fall into disrepair. In 1719, the Castle Hotel was built on the site.

**Tong Castle:** This Gothic-style country house was originally built some time in the 1100s. It is listed as Tong Tuange in Domesday Book, held by Roger de Montgomery, Earl of Shrewsbury, and was subsequently owned by the de Harcourts, the de Pembridges and the Vernons. During the English Civil War the castle was garrisoned for the king by William Carless, and then by George Mainwaring. The original castle was knocked down in 1765 to allow an impressive mansion to be built, and that year the house passed from the Durant family to the Earl of Bradford, who let out the house. Extensive fire damage in 1911 rendered the house unstable and therefore uninhabitable. The ruins were knocked down between 1954 and 1956 in the name of progress to make way for the new M54 motorway.

**Ruyton-of-the-Eleven-Towns Castle:** Situated within the uniquely named Ruyton-XI-Towns/Ruyton of the Eleven Towns or simply Ruyton if you prefer, the castle is thought to have been built by John de Strange some time in the twelfth century. In 1148, Fulk FitzWarine destroyed the castle, which was then rebuilt before the Welsh destroyed it again. Rebuilt again some time before 1313, it was subsequently acquired by Roger Mortimer, Earl of March, but abandoned after 1364, and fell into ruin. The town was formed by a charter in 1310.

**Ellesmere Castle:** A motte and bailey thought to have been built by Roger de Montgomery a little after 1086, it became a royal castle in 1138, but was abandoned in the fourteenth century. Nothing remains of the castle itself.

The county has a great many mottes, and mottes and baileys. Here are just a few: Middlehope Castle, Lydham, More, Near Hyssington, Near Lower Down, Hardwick, Near Nantcribba, Wotherton, East Dudston, Near Poundback and Brompton Bridge.

# 20

# ABBEYS AND CHURCHES

**Buildwas Abbey:** Located on the banks of the Severn about 2 miles west of Ironbridge, the Cistercian Abbey of St Mary and St Chad was originally founded in 1135 by Roger de Clinton, Bishop of Coventry (1129–48). It was a Savignac monastery inhabited by a small community of six to twelve monks, who made their income by charging tolls to passing travellers on the bridge over the Severn. The abbey's location near the Welsh border meant it had a turbulent history. The Welsh regularly raided the abbey and, on one occasion in 1406, kidnapped the abbot. In 1342 one of the monks, Thomas Tong, murdered his abbot, and evaded arrest before cheekily petitioning for re-instatement into the Cistercian order. The abbey closed in 1536, during Henry VIII's Dissolution of the Monasteries, and the estate was granted to Lord Powis, the abbot's house and infirmary later being incorporated into a private house. The abbey ruins are under the care of English Heritage. Although it has no roof, the church is one of the best-preserved twelfth-century Cistercian churches in Britain.

**Haughmond Abbey:** Four miles from Shrewsbury, Haughmond is sometimes referred to as the Abbey of St John the Evangelist. Of the three houses of Austin canons established in Shropshire, Haughmond, founded in 1135 by William Fitz Alan, is the oldest. The abbey occupies a beautiful setting on the sloping site of Haughmond Hill. The richly coloured mellowed stone of the ruined parts of the chapter house, refectory and the fourteenth-century infirmary are still viewable, but only the foundations of the abbey church remain. Close by on the hill is the spot known as Douglas's Leap – where the Earl of Douglas, in flight from the

Battle of Shrewsbury, was thrown from his horse and captured by Henry IV's men. Set into the arches of the chapter house are a series of intricate carvings of saints thought to be Augustine, Thomas Beckett, Catherine of Alexandria, John the Evangelist, John the Baptist, Margaret of Antioch, Winifred and Michael. There are also a number of tombstones, plus an octagonal font. When the abbey was dissolved in 1539, there were ten canons and an abbot in residence. The abbey passed to Sir Edward Littlejohn and later Sir Rowland Hill and the Barker family. The site is now in the care of English Heritage.

**Lilleshall Abbey:** The remains of this twelfth- and thirteenth-century medieval monastery, the church, and other large domestic buildings can still be seen. However, other buildings, such as a lady chapel and canon's dormitory, have long since disappeared. The abbey was enclosed by a large precinct wall, a little of which still survives. It is thought that the abbey was founded by Richard de Belmeis, who settled a group of Arrouasian (later Augustinian) canons there around 1148. Income came from farming and two water mills, the rest from properties in Shrewsbury and from tolls from Atcham Bridge, but by the early fourteenth century the abbey was heavily in debt. Following its dissolution in around 1538, when in addition to the abbot and nine canons, there were forty-three servants and a schoolmaster living there, the property and its goods were sold for £75 to the Cavendish family, who passed it a year later to James Leveson of Wolverhampton. During the English Civil War, the abbey was fortified for King Charles I by Sir Richard Leveson, and afterwards fell into ruins. In 1950 the abbey came into the ownership of the Office of Works and was later repaired before coming into the care of English Heritage.

**Shrewsbury Abbey:** Founded in 1083 by the Norman Roger de Montgomery, the abbey started life modestly as the small wooden Saxon Chapel of St Peter, whose priest, on returning from a pilgrimage to Rome, persuaded Earl Roger to transform the church into an abbey. Roger agreed and sent for two monks from Normandy to direct the construction. When completed the new building became the centre of Norman power in the region. For 457 years the abbey was populated by Benedictine monks and flourished during the early twelfth century. All that was missing were a few religious relics, so the abbot sent Prior Robert Pennant to Wales to find something suitable. Pennant returned in 1138 with the bones of Saint Gwenfrewi (St Winifred), a seventh-century Welsh martyr. The relics enshrined, Shrewsbury Abbey became a major centre of pilgrimage. A parliament met in the chapter house in 1283. The Dissolution of the Monasteries changed much of the abbey and its buildings, the shortened nave being left to serve as the parish church.

Today Shrewsbury Abbey stands on a large, harp-shaped green, surrounded by trees and gravestones. The fourteenth-century west tower, with its large decorated stained-glass window, has a statue of King Edward II. The remains of four of the huge drum-shaped columns from the original Norman church can still be seen, together with fragments of Saint Winifred's shrine. The First World War memorial below the tower includes the name of war poet Lieutenant W.E.S. Owen, MC (Wilfred Owen), killed in action in 1918.

**Wenlock Priory:** The spectacular ruins of Wenlock Priory are the remains of a twelfth-century church that belonged to the Cluniac monastery, refounded in 1079 and 1082, on the site of an earlier seventh-century foundation by Roger de Montgomery. It is thought to be the final resting place of Saint Milburga, whose bones were discovered during restoration work in 1101. Merewalh, King of the Magonsaete (a mini-kingdom within the Anglo-Saxon Kingdom of Mercia) founded the original Anglo-Saxon monastery here in AD 680. His daughter became its abbess. She was later canonised, and died in AD 727. The priory was only inhabited by monks after the Norman Conquest. In the early fourteenth century, the 350ft long priory church was completely rebuilt, the remains of which include the north and south transepts and the nave. Following the Dissolution in 1540, several buildings, including the late fifteenth-century prior's house, were converted into private residences.

**Whiteladies Priory:** Built on the grounds of a medieval nunnery, it was to White Ladies that Charles II was taken after fleeing from defeat at Worcester. He arrived on Thursday, 4 September 1651 after a nightlong ride, and was admitted to the house by a servant named George Penderel.

The name 'White Ladies' refers to the white (undyed) habits of the nuns who lived there. The large timber-framed nunnery has long since disappeared; all that remains are the ruins of the medieval church and the nineteenth-century boundary wall of the small graveyard. The priory is located about a mile from Boscobel House (the grounds include the famous Royal Oak, where Charles II hid briefly). The priory is also rumoured to be where Queen Guinevere retired after the death of King Arthur.

ST LAURENCE'S CHURCH

# 21

# HILLS AND VALLEYS

The Shropshire landscape is wide and varied, and offers some of the most spectacular and delightful scenery in the country, all resting on the most extraordinary geological foundations. About 420 million years ago, give or take a few minutes, much of Shropshire was 4,000 miles away from where it is now. Believe it or not, the county was situated south of the Equator, but not only that – it was several fathoms under the sea, where the mineral-rich Stiperstones, and limestone areas around south Shropshire were created, and in the north of the county, glaciers deposited clay, gravel and sand to create Shropshire's very own lake district. The wonderfully undulating terrain of the Shropshire hills: Caer Caradoc, the Long Mynd and the Stiperstones, together with the Clee hills, give that part of the county an alpine feel, especially when there is snow on their summits. But let's start with the Wrekin.

**The Wrekin:** Heavily featured in legend and folklore, this imposing hill in the middle of an otherwise flattish landscape rises to 1,335ft (407m) (my dad told me it was a field with its back up!) The Wrekin is a magnificent sight, and from its summit it is claimed that it's possible to see fifteen different counties; mind you, it has to be a clear day. It has been suggested that the Wrekin inspired J.R.R. Tolkien's Middle Earth in his *The Lord of the Rings* series (see Legends).

Almost everyone I have ever spoken to knows the phrase 'Going round the Wrekin', meaning to go out of your way to do or say something.

**The Long Mynd:** A large and long plateau with steep valleys and escarpments covering an area of over 8.5 square miles (22 sq. km), much of the Long Mynd is owned by the National Trust. A sea of purple heather in late summer, the name means 'Long Mountain' – in Welsh it is 'Mynydd Hir'. The Mynd towers over Church Stretton and at Pole Bank it rises to a height of 1,693ft (516m). The 5-mile long ancient trackway the Portway runs the length of the Long Mynd massif. In the Precambrian era it would have been 60° south of the Equator.

**The Clee Hills:** This 15-mile-long range consists of the Brown Clee, Abdon Burf (the highest peak at 1,792ft (546m), often recorded as 1,772ft (540m), but either way the tallest hill in the county) and another peak is Clee Burf. Titterstone Clee Hill at 1,749ft (546m) is another in the range all created in the last Ice Age, which peaked about 21,000 million years ago and ended about 11,500 million years ago.

**Stiperstones:** A spectacular 10km ridge on which Manston Rock at 1,759ft (536m) is the second-highest hill in Shropshire – another place of mystery and legend. Formed 480 million years ago, this quartzite ridge is 5 miles long, crowned by a number of jagged rocky outcrops surrounded by a sea of heather: Manstone Rock, The Devils Chair, Shepherd Rock, The Rock, Nipstone Rock and Cranberry Rock. The area was a mining centre for centuries.

**Caer Caradoc:** With an impressive elevation of 1,506ft (459m), this imposing hill could be called the baby brother of the Long Mynd. It lies to the east of the A49, dominating the countryside. On the top of the hill is an Iron Age hill fort claimed to be where Caratacus, the chieftain of the Catuvellauni tribe, fought his final battle against the Roman invaders in AD 50.

**Nesscliffe Hill:** The sandstone escarpment of Nesscliffe Hill near Ruyton is now a designated country park with a number of trails through the woods. The outline of the ramparts of an old hill fort are to be found on the north side of the hill. The spectacular cliff face of the old sandstone quarry contains the supposed hideout of the notorious highwayman Sir Humphrey Kynaston and his horse, Beelzebub.

**Wenlock Edge:** Millions of years ago, reefs of coral skeletons, sea lilies and sponges were formed in the shallow subtropical waters mentioned earlier, a reef that is known today as Wenlock Edge – one of the most magnificent escarpments in the entire country. Amazingly, nine species of orchid grow there.

**The Lawley:** One of the most picturesque of the South Shropshire Hills, the Lawley lies alongside the A49, a little north of Caer Caradoc, rising to around 1,200ft (370m).

# 22

# TRANSPORT

In 1800, the Holyhead mail coach left London at 8 p.m. and took twenty-seven hours to reach Shrewsbury. The 162-mile journey across rutted and uneven roads was made by way of Oxford. In the same year, the Shrewsbury and Chester High Flyer covered the 40 miles between the two towns in twelve hours. By 1831, both these journey times had been cut dramatically: to around sixteen and a half hours from London to Shrewsbury, and less than four hours from Shrewsbury to Chester.

**The Severn Valley Railway:** Take a trip down memory lane on the wonderful 16-mile long Severn Valley Railway's steam and diesel trains running between Bridgnorth and Kidderminster. At the Highley stop there is the Engine House Visitor Centre, which houses

some fantastic steam locomotives and rolling stock. Along the Severn Valley route there are a number of picturesque stations – my favourite is at Arley. The original line opened in 1862 and went from Shrewsbury to Hartlebury in Worcestershire.

**The Royal Air Force Museum:** RAF Cosford's fabulous museum houses a huge collection of warplanes, rockets and civil aeroplanes, plus an exhibition hangar dedicated to the Cold War.

Talking of aeroplanes, following the Wright brothers' first recorded flight on 17 December 1903, two Shropshire men were amongst the early pioneers of powered flight in this country. Arthur Phillips of Market Drayton was an engineer and maker of bicycles fascinated by flight. He built the British Matchless Convertiplane in 1908. The other is Ernest Maund of Craven Arms, claimed to be the first man to fly in Shropshire, though this accolade has subsequently been disputed. Maund is said to have taken off from a field at Stokesay some time between 1904 and 1907. There is a photograph of the aviator sitting high up in the cockpit of a monoplane aircraft, flanked by his two sisters and with a sign that proclaims 'Briton No. 1'. The aeroplane is believed to have been purchased at auction, sold by world speed ace Malcolm Campbell, who had decided to concentrate on the land and water speed records after a couple of disappointing flights in Kent in 1909 and 1910.

It would be remiss not to mention the invention of the world's first passenger steam locomotive and the men responsible for it in more detail.

**Richard Trevithick (1771–1833):** Born 13 April 1771 in Tregajorran, near Pool in Cornwall, the 6ft 2in engineer Richard Trevithick invented the steam locomotive, not, as many believe, George Stephenson (1781–1848). Trevithick is famous in

Shropshire as the man responsible for the locomotive *Catch Me Who Can*, built in 1808 at the Rastrick and Hazeldine works in Bridgnorth. This was his fourth railway steam locomotive, following earlier locos at Coalbrookdale, Penydarren and Wylam.

The son of a Cornish mining captain, Trevithick was fascinated by the steam engines that pumped water from tin and copper mines. He married Jane Harvey, whose blacksmith father formed his own company making condensing or atmospheric beam engines for pumping water (also known as low-pressure engines), which were invented by Thomas Newcomen in 1712 (the famous James Watt held patents for efficiency improvements). In 1797, Trevithick went to work as engineer for the Ding Dong Mine and, with Edward Bull, pioneered the use of high-pressure steam. Trevithick was introduced to the potential of 'strong steam' by William Murdock in 1794, and experimented in harnessing steam at high pressures, resulting in lighter, more compact engines. He built a stationary engine, then attached it to a carriage. In 1801, Trevithick built a full-size locomotive, which he named the 'Puffing Devil', and successfully transported six passengers from Camborne to the village of Beacon. In 1802, he took out a patent for his engine, and that year built a static engine at the Coalbrookdale Company in Shropshire. His next project, in 1803, was another locomotive: the 'London Steam Carriage', which was driven from Holborn to Paddington and back. That year a static engine of his at Greenwich exploded, killing four men; faulty operation rather than faulty machinery was blamed.

In 1808, Trevithick designed and built a new locomotive named *Catch Me Who Can* at the factory in Bridgnorth, owned by John Hazeldine and John Urpeth Rastrick, which he ran successfully on a circular track near present-day Euston Station he called the 'Steam Circus', charging 1s admission including a ride. The locomotive reached a top speed of 12mph (19km/h), but unfortunately the engine proved too heavy for the brittle track, and a broken cast-iron rail caused a derailment, forcing Trevithick to close his exhibition. Disappointed, Trevithick decided this was to be his last railway locomotive and in May 1810, he almost died of typhoid. In 1812, Matthew Murray finally built a competitive twin-cylinder locomotive. Trevithick went on to build engines for multiple purposes: stone crushing, forge hammers, blast furnace blowers, barges with paddle wheels and dredgers. Then in 1816,

# TREVITHICKS.
## PORTABLE STEAM ENGINE.

Catch me who can.

Mechanical Power Subduing
Animal Speed. JKS

Trevithick travelled to South America for a business ventures which failed, forcing him to serve in the forces of revolutionary Simon Bolivar, returning to England almost destitute in 1827. More inventions followed, but in 1833 he contracted pneumonia, and died on 22 April. He was buried in Dartford, where he was working at the time.

The revolutionary mechanical arrangement of Trevithick's new engine design was simpler, with the cylinder mounted in a vertical position, the flywheel and gears encased within the boiler, driving the pair of rear wheels by connecting rods.

A replica of the *Catch Me Who Can* locomotive was built at Bridgnorth's Severn Valley Railway.

**William Hazeldine (or Hazledine) (1763–1840):** Hazeldine was a master structural engineer and ironmaster almost unknown among the great innovators of the Industrial Revolution. A collaborator and contemporary of the great engineer Thomas Telford, Hazeldine was born in Waters Upton, Shropshire in 1763, and at the time of his death was spoken of as the foremost practical man in Europe. Along with partner John Urpeth Rastrick, Hazeldine's factories provided the ironwork for five of the world's 'firsts': Ditherington Flax Mill at Shrewsbury, the world's first iron-framed building; Pontcysyllte Aqueduct, near Chirk, still one of the longest and highest aqueducts in Britain; the lock gates on the wonderful Caledonian Canal; a new genre of cast-iron arch bridge; and the Menai Suspension Bridge, which joins Anglesey to the Welsh mainland. Hazeldine contributed greatly to the development of mills and millwrighting in Shropshire and surrounding counties. Richard Trevithick's *Catch Me Who Can* steam locomotive was built at the Bridgnorth foundry of Rastrick and Hazeldine.

The Hazeldine & Co. iron foundry was situated at the bottom of Bandon Lane in Low Town, Bridgnorth. It was set up around 1792 to manufacture cast-iron agricultural implements on the eastern bank of the River Severn in Bridgnorth by three Hazeldine brothers: John (1760–1810), Robert (1768–1837) and Thomas (1771–1842). A fourth brother, William (1763–1840), had already established a flourishing independent ironworks business in Shrewsbury, and collaborated with many engineers, including Thomas Telford (1757–1834) and Richard Trevithick.

In November 1949, the innovative part that Richard Trevithick, William Hazeldine and John Rastrick played in the Industrial Revolution was commemorated by a bronze plaque on the red-brick clock tower at the east end of Telford's bridge over the River Severn at Bridgnorth. The text reads:

TO THE MEMORY OF TWO GREAT ENGINEERS RICHARD
TREVITHICK B. 1771 – D. 1833 INVENTOR OF THE HIGH
PRESSURE STEAM ENGINE AND JOHN URPETH RASTRICK
B. 1780 – D. 1856 GREAT RAILWAY ENGINEER. NEAR THIS
SPOT IN HAZELDINE'S FOUNDRY RASTRICK BUILT IN 1808
TO TREVITHICK'S DESIGN THE WORLD'S FIRST PASSENGER
LOCOMOTIVE ENGINE.

To mark the bicentenary of *Catch Me Who Can*, another plaque
was unveiled in Bandon Lane, Bridgnorth. It bears an image of the
locomotive and the text:

ON THIS SITE STOOD HAZELDINE'S FOUNDRY WHERE IN 1808
WAS BUILT THE WORLD'S FIRST STEAM LOCOMOTIVE TO
HAUL FEE-PAYING PASSENGERS. THIS ENGINE WAS DESIGNED
BY RICHARD TREVITHICK, ENGINEERED BY JOHN RASTRICK
AND BUILT BY THE FOUNDRY WORKERS OF BRIDGNORTH. THIS
PLAQUE WAS ERECTED BY BRIDGNORTH CIVIC SOCIETY
FUNDED MAINLY BY MEMBER MRS. CHRISTINA HOLDER
AND ADDITIONALLY BY: BRIDGNORTH TOWN COUNCIL,
BRIDGNORTH DISTRICT COUNCIL, BRIDGNORTH TOURIST
ASSOCIATION IN JULY 2008.

# 23

# DISASTERS, ACCIDENTS AND TRAGEDIES

Sadly, Shropshire has seen its fair share of mining accidents:

In 1810, thirteen men plus a number of pit ponies escaped death at the Meadow Pit at Blists Hill when an underground fire swept through the tunnels. During an inspection the following day, four men died from carbon monoxide poisoning.

At the Pitchcroft Limestone mine on Lilleshall Hill, three men were crushed to death by falling stone in 1858.

At the Brick Kiln Leasow Pit, Madeley, nine men were killed in 1864 when the chain winding gear failed, plunging the men to their death.

In the Springwell Pit disaster at Holly Lane, Little Dawley, on Friday, 6 December 1872 eight men lost their lives. This was the first such tragedy in the Dawley area, although nine men had been killed in the Dark Lane Pit accident in 1862. It followed another incident at Pelsall in Staffordshire where twenty-two men, including five Dawley colliers, were killed. The accident happened when a chain snapped as the men were being hauled to the surface.

In 1875 at Lodgebank Colliery in Donnington Wood, eleven men and one pony were suffocated to death after breathing in toxic gases following an underground fire. The mine was later nicknamed 'Slaughter Pit'.

The George's Shaft Accident took place in the Snailbeach Mine at about 6.15 a.m. on 6 March 1895, claiming the lives of seven miners when the steel winding cable carrying their cage failed, plunging the men to their death. Earlier that morning, the system had been successfully raised and lowered for three test runs, and had been used twice to carry cages of night-shift workers. The verdict of the subsequent inquest was of accidental death due to a defective rope. This accident also claimed the life of Anne Blower, the wife of a miner *not* involved, who collapsed and died after being wrongly informed of her husband's death.

Another rope breakage at the same mine in 1897 caused a cage to plunge to the bottom of the shaft, but fortunately this time it was empty.

Lead was mined at Snailbeach from at least Roman times, evidenced by the discovery of a Roman ingot. When the Romans went back home, mining ceased and the mine was left derelict for centuries until the sixteenth century. Mining continued until 1955 when the mine closed for good.

On 4 December 1910 at the Kemberton Pit, near Madeley, five men and two boys were crushed to death, again the result of winding gear failure.

To give some idea of scale of the danger of local mining:

- Between 1878 and 1969, twenty men were killed at Highley Colliery.
- Between 1871 and 1921, three men were killed at Billingsley Colliery.
- Between 1892 and 1936, eleven men were killed at Kinlet Colliery.
- Between 1922 and 1928, one man was killed at Chorley Drift.
- Between 1935 and 1969, eight men were killed at Alveley Colliery.

## NEAR TRAGEDY ON THE LONG MYND

On the Long Mynd in January 1865, the Victorian clergyman Reverend E. Donald Carr, rector of Woolstaston church, found himself lost in a snow blizzard. He nearly plunged to his death into the Light Spout Waterfall, which becomes a spectacular 4m cascading waterfall following prolonged rainfall.

Every Sunday for nearly ten years, having given morning service and eaten his lunch, Reverend Carr would ride the 4 miles from

Woolstaston to Ratlinghope church to give the afternoon service. The ride took him across the highest and most exposed part of the Long Mynd hills. On this January day in 1865, the fog was dense and deep snow covered the ground, but the dutiful clergyman decided to go ahead. Wearing a light coat, he and his servant set off on horseback in a snowstorm, but soon found their horses struggling. Undeterred, Carr sent his servant back with the horses and continued on foot through thigh-deep drifts, tugging away the slugs of ice that formed on his legs, and at times crawling on hands and knees. His arrival at Rattlinghope at 3.30 p.m. raised the eyebrows of the tiny congregation, to whom he gave a short service before starting out on the return journey. He was begged to stay the night, but declined, saying he needed to get back to Woolstaston to give the evening service. That return journey nearly cost him his life.

The storm had become even more ferocious, and now peppered his face with ice and sleet, forcing him to look down, but as he crossed the summit he lost his way. Stumbling, he then lost his footing and suddenly found himself hurtling down a steep slope, with the prospect of death of the rocks below. He dug in his heels, arresting his death slide on the edge of a crag, from where he inched his way to the valley below. He now found himself in a 20ft deep drift, but managed to crawl out. Hat and gloves gone, and with night approaching, the tired, hungry, lost and frostbitten clergyman climbed and climbed only to fall back to the valley once again. Worse still, when he tried to look at his watch he realised he was suffering from snow blindness. A semblance of daylight brought no relief. He followed a stream and almost plunged into the Light Spout Waterfall. By the afternoon of the second day the reverend was almost totally exhausted, and as if things couldn't get worse, his boots came off; he tried to carry them but could not. Struggling through shoulder-deep drifts he heard the sound of children playing. He had reached the Carding Mill Valley. All but one of the children ran away when they heard his cries for help, seeing only the scary outline of an ice-covered figure. An inquisitive girl took a closer look, and recognised the preacher. He was taken first to a cottage, then to Church Stretton, where a doctor tended to him before allowing him to be taken home, where following a period of recuperation he made a full recovery.

Reverend Carr's epic ordeal is a triumph of one man's strength of will and determination, born out of his proud boast that whatever the weather he had never once missed a service and his confidence that, having holidayed in the Alps, he would know what to expect and how to deal with adverse conditions. The vicar's boots are now held by the Shropshire Museums Service.

## AIR CRASH

A tragic air crash happened on 19 August 1944 at Leebotwood, Shropshire, when the pilot lost control of his aircraft, thought to be as a result of turbulence, resulting in a wing becoming detached. The aeroplane was a Mosquito KB224 from RAF 1655 Mosquito training unit. Sadly the pilot, Flight Lieutenant J.M. Pearce, and Pilot Officer A.A. Young were both killed. In 2007, when the plane was excavated, a 500-ton bomb was discovered and detonated on the spot.

## RAIL DISASTERS

**The Rednal rail crash:** On 7 June 1865, an excursion train from Birkenhead via Chester to Shrewsbury crashed 600yds north of Rednal Station, just south of Whittington, near Oswestry. A thirty-two-carriage train and two brake vans were being pulled by two locomotives. Workmen packing up the rails had set up a warning flag at the top of a steep gradient over 1,000yds from where they were working, which the driver of the locomotive failed to see. When he saw the workmen, the driver slammed on the brakes, but it was too late. The leading locomotive left the un-packed rails, careering along at speed to Rednal Station, where it overturned, destroying the first four carriages. Sadly, eleven passengers and two crewmembers were killed.

**The Shrewsbury rail crash:** On 15 October 1907, on the sharp bend coming into Shrewsbury Station, a fifteen-carriage, overnight sleeping car and mail train (number 2052 – Stephenson, from Manchester) left the tracks, killing the driver and fireman, two guards, eleven passengers and three Post Office mail sorters. Thirty-three other people were reported injured. It was believed that the train was travelling at around 60mph on a bend with a 10mph limit, and that the driver must have dozed off.

**Coton Hill rail crash:** On 11 January 1965, the driver of a freight train failed to obey a stop signal and lost control on the steep Hencote Incline. The train accelerated to 20mph as it derailed, demolishing a signal box, killing the signalman, and seriously injuring its driver before it came to a stop. One other man was slightly injured.

**The Welshampton rail crash:** On 11 June 1897, a fifteen-carriage, two-locomotive excursion train carrying 320 passengers from Barmouth back home to Royton, Oldham, derailed as it neared Welshampton Station, west of Ellesmere, killing nine passengers, two others and a railway employee, who died subsequently.

**The Baschurch Station crash:** On 13 February 1961, the locomotive of the Wellington to Chester Express was travelling at a little over 40mph when it struck a freight train that had been shunted to allow the express to pass through, but was still partially obstructing the main line. The express locomotive struck a glancing blow to the front of the freight train, overturning between the platforms. At the front of the express was a railway stores van with two storemen inside. The van and passenger carriage caught fire. The crash killed the driver and fireman of the express, and a storeman; the second storeman was seriously injured. The other injured were the driver, fireman and guard of the freight train, plus the guard from the express. Two of the twenty-two passengers were slightly injured.

In January 1858, the driver of a coal train stepped down from his cab to open the gates at Priors Lee level crossing, but he had left the engine in gear and had forgotten to apply the brake. His own locomotive crushed him to death.

October 1875 saw the death of another train driver at Potts Yard, Abbey Foregate. A locomotive had been shunting in the yard when three of the wagons began to run down the slope, towards another train of fourteen wagons that was proceeding up the slope. The driver of the second train slammed on his brakes only to be crushed to death in the collision.

# 24

# WARTIME SHROPSHIRE

In 1914 the army requisitioned the best horses at Minsterley for use as cavalry mounts, and heavy horses for pulling wagons and guns. Remount centres were set up at Whixall Moss and at Craven Arms. Sadly, over 256,000 horses and mules died on the Western Front. Not many made it home: some were sold as workhorses, others as meat.

In April 1915, Stokesay Court was set up as an auxiliary military hospital.

In 1918 a wooden hut housing thirty-five sleeping men was set on fire at Bent Lane Conscientious Objector Camp in Ditton Priors. Fortunately no one was injured. The men were labourers at Brown Clee Quarry.

In the early hours of 29 August 1940, a German bomber jettisoned its murderous load from the skies above Shropshire. The bombs, twelve in all, fell on the historic town of Bridgnorth. One landed where Listley Street joins St Mary's Street, not far from the Squirrel Hotel (now Whitburn Grange), leaving a massive crater. A sweetshop across the road was blown up. Other bombs landed at the back of shops in the High Street, in Church Street and near St Leonard's church. Sadly, two women were killed and seven people injured in the raid. German bombs also fell on Crewe Bank in Shrewsbury.

On 26 June 1940, five bombs fell on Shawbury. There were no casualties, but properties were damaged.

On 25 August 1940, bombs falling at Newcastle-on-Clun caused no casualties, but damaged a cottage.

3 August 1940, at Sambrook, an unexploded bomb caused the village pub to close – the army blew the bomb up, and there were no casualties.

31 August 1940, bombs killed three people in Shrewsbury.

5 September 1940, the fire brigade at Bishop's Castle had a narrow escape when German bombs fell on their station while they were out tackling a blaze in Churchstoke.

15 September 1940, bombs blew out all the windows at the Citadel, the home of Lady Stanier, at Hawkstone.

On the night of 28 September 1940, the blast from a German bomb left behind a huge crater on Lilleshall Golf Course.

10 October 1940, the Luftwaffe bombed Shrewsbury.

Early on the morning of 16 October 1940, sixteen bombs were dropped near Longnor. The same day, a German plane strafed a goods train near Yockleton, hitting the tail lamps on the guard's van.

22 October 1940, a bomb made a large crater between Caradoc and Little Caradoc.

26 October 1940, during a daring daylight raid, the Allscott Sugar Beet factory was damaged.

9 November 1940, an air raid over Ironbridge put a stop to the mayoral investiture proceedings. There were no casualties, but the home of the town clerk was damaged, among others.

On the night of 15 November 1940, a Heinkel He 111 German bomber crashed at Derrington, between Ditton Priors and Monkhampton. The Luftwaffe pilot, Karl Svata, and one other crewmember, navigator Alfred Achstaller, parachuted to safety, landing in fields near Spoonhill Wood. After dropping their bombs over Birmingham, they were flying over south-east Shropshire when the wings iced up and the plane went into a steep dive and began to break up.

THE HEATH CHAPEL

The night of 28 November 1940 saw the largest air raid over Shropshire, when the Luftwaffe dropped an estimated twenty-seven high-explosive bombs, more than 100 incendiary bombs and eight parachute mines, causing a great deal of damage in Cruckmoor Lane, Prees Lower Heath and Tugford church.

A bizarre incident occurred on Berwick Road, Shrewsbury, after a raid during the evening of 2 December 1940: a German bomb left a huge crater into which a lady motorist drove her car.

On 12 July 1941 a German prisoner threw a rock at a guard at Oswestry POW Camp, who then shot the prisoner dead.

Over 2,000 wartime egg collection posts were set up in the UK – 500,000 eggs were needed each week for wounded soldiers and sailors in hospitals overseas – hen, duck, goose and even plover eggs were sent packed in crates of sawdust. Any broken eggs went to feed the wounded in the UK. Collection Post number 330 was at Much Wenlock.

## POW CAMPS IN SHROPSHIRE

During the First World War a number of camps were set up in the county of Shropshire to house German POWs, at Bromfield, Clee Hill Ddu, Cleobury Mortimer, Corfdon Hall, Ellesmere and at Mile House, near Oswestry.

During the Second World War, Shropshire had eighteen POW camps, at Acksea; Kinnerley (camp 34, later renamed camp 1018); Adderley Hall, near Market Drayton (camp 109); Cluddley, Wellington (camp 1004); Condover Airfield Camp, near Shrewsbury; Davenport House, near Worfield (camp 272); Donnington near Wellington housed three camps, South (camp 651), North (camp 659), and E' (camp 1004); Green Fields; Hawkstone Park, Weston (camp 240); Merrington Green; Mile House, near Oswestry (camp 8); Prees Heath Alien Internment Camp, near Whitchurch (camp 16); Sheets Farm, Sheet (camp 84); Sheriffhales (camp 71); St Martins, Bank Top, Oswestry (camp 100); Wem (camp 679); Wilcott, Nesscliffe (camp 591).

## WARTIME PRODUCTION

During the war Shrewsbury produced aircraft parts at Wales and Edwards, Prees; armaments (shell casings, parts for Bren guns and

SPITFIRE

machine tools were made at the Sentinel Factory), wings for Spitfire fighter aircraft and other aircraft parts. The garage on London Road produced Spitfire wings and fuselages; Centurion tanks were also made in Shrewsbury. Radio Gramophone development took place at a Ministry of Aircraft factory in Bridgnorth. Camouflage netting was made in Bridgnorth at the Rootes Securities factory; fuel tanks for aircraft at Peaton and there was a munitions factory in Coalbrookdale in 1913.

# MUSICAL SHROPSHIRE

Ian Hunter of the rock band Mott the Hoople was born Ian Hunter Patterson in Oswestry, on 3 June 1939. The band's most famous hits were 'All the Young Dudes' and 'Roll away the Stone'.

Ozzy Osbourne once owned Ozzy's Wine Bar in St Mary's Street, Newport.

K.K. Downing of the heavy metal band Judas Priest owns and lives in Astbury Hall, near Bridgnorth.

The band T'Pau hailed from Shropshire although their singer, Carol Decker, was born in Huyton, Liverpool. She was, however, educated in Wellington, as were most of the other band members. The band's biggest hit was 'China in Your Hand'.

Opera singer Isobel Cooper was born in Much Wenlock.

# EDUCATION

Many famous people have attended the equally famous Shrewsbury School. Originally a boarding school for boys, Shrewsbury School was founded by Royal Charter in 1552, moving to its present campus in 1882. Now an independent co-educational school, its pupils are known as Old Salopians. Among the most notable are:

- Elizabethan poet and statesman Sir Philip Sydney (1554–86)
- Naturalist and father of today's views on evolution Charles Darwin (1809–82)
- Astronomer Royal Martin Rees (1942–)
- Author Samuel Butler (1835–1902)
- Broadcaster and DJ John Peel (1939–2004)
- Author Nevil Shute (1899–1960)
- Python and world traveller Michael Palin CBE (1943–)
- Television presenter Nick Owen (1947–)
- Broadcaster Nick Hancock (1962–)
- Judge Lord Hutton (1931–)
- Humourist Willie Rushton (1937–96)
- Journalists and founders of the magazine *Private Eye*: Richard Ingrams (1937–), and Christopher Booker (1937–)
- Politician the Right Honourable Lord Hestletine, CH, PC (1933–)
- Mountaineer Andrew Irvine (1902–24)
- Judge George Jeffreys, 1st Baron Jeffreys (1645–89)

# POSTSCRIPT

Well, as they say at the end of Warner Bros. cartoons: tha ... tha ... tha ... that's all folks!

I hope you enjoyed the read.

## ALSO BY JOHN SHIPLEY
## WITH THE HISTORY PRESS

*Wolves Against the World – European Nights 1953–1980*
*Wolverhampton Wanderers Champions 1953/54*
*Nottingham Forest Champions 1977/78*
*Aston Villa Champions 1980/81*
*The Nottingham Forest Miscellany*

Also from The History Press

# WHEN DISASTER STRIKES